This item is due for return on or before the last date stamped below.
Charges will be made for late return. Items may be renewed by
telephone quoting either the barcode number or your library card
number.

Do you know you can also renew your books, search the library
catalogue and reserve items via the Internet? Just go to
www.bexley.gov.uk/library and click on 'e-Library'. You will need your
library card number and PIN.

What's in it for schools?
Edited by Kate Myers and John MacBeath

Inspection: What's in it for schools?
James Learmonth

Inspection

What's in it for schools?

James Learmonth

London and New York

First published 2000
by RoutledgeFalmer
11 New Fetter Lane, London EC4P 4EE

Simultaneously published in the USA and Canada
by RoutledgeFalmer
29 West 35th Street, New York, NY 10001

RoutledgeFalmer is an imprint of the Taylor & Francis Group

© 2000 James Learmonth

Typeset in Baskerville by
M Rules
Printed and bound in Great Britain by Clays Ltd, St Ives plc

British Library Cataloguing in Publication Data
A catalogue record for this book is available from the British
Library

Library of Congress Cataloging in Publication Data
Learmonth, James, 1939–
    Inspection: what's in it for schools? / James Learmonth.
        p. cm. — (What's in it for schools?)
    Includes bibliographical references (p.) and index.
    1. School management and organization— Great Britain.
    2. School improvement programs—Great Britain. 3.
    Schools—Great Britain—Evaluation. I. Title. II. Series.
    LB2900.5 .L47 2000
    379.1′58′0941—dc21   00-059207

ISBN 0 415 22784 4 (hbk)
ISBN 0 415 22785 2 (pbk)

Many shall run to and fro, and knowledge shall increase.

Daniel 12: 4

'Sir, please can you come again next week? We do ever such interesting work when you're here.'

(Pupil to inspector: SW London secondary school, 1990)

WHY A NEW EDUCATION CODE IS NEEDED.

Inspector. "I AM VERY SORRY TO SAY, MISS WILKINS, THAT NOT ONE CHILD IN THIS STANDARD CAN EXPLAIN THE 'EXTENDED PREDICATE!'"

Contents

Figures

Tables

Series Editors' preface

Kate Myers and John MacBeath

Series introduction

There is a concerted move to raise standards in the public education system. The aim is laudable. Few people would disagree with it. However, there is no clear agreement about what we mean by 'standards'. Do we mean attainment or achievement more broadly defined, for example, and how we are to raise whatever it is we agree needs raising?

At the same time, there appears to be an increasing trend towards approaching changes in education through a controlling, rational and technical framework. This framework tends to concentrate on educational content and delivery and ignores the human resource perspective and the complexity of how human beings live, work and interact with one another. It overemphasises linearity and pays insufficient attention to how people respond to change and either support or subvert it.

Recent government initiatives, including the National Curriculum, OFSTED school and LEA inspections, assessment procedures, league tables, target-setting, literacy and numeracy hours, and performance management have endorsed this framework. On occasions this has been less to do with the content of 'reforms' than the process of implementation – that is, doing it 'to' rather than 'with' the teaching profession. Teachers are frequently treated as the problem rather than part of the solution, with the consequence that many feel disillusioned, demoralised and disempowered. Critics of this *top-down* approach are often seen as lacking rigour, complacent about standards, and uninterested in raising achievement.

We wanted to edit this series because we believe that you can be passionate about public education, about raising achievement, about ensuring that all pupils are entitled to the best possible education that society is able to provide – whatever their race, sex or class. We also believe that achieving this is not a simple matter of common sense or of the appliance of science – it is more complex than that. Most of all, we see the teaching profession as an important part of the solution to finding ways through these complexities.

What's in it for schools? is a series that will make educational policy issues relevant to practitioners. Each book in the series focuses on a major educational issue and raises key questions, such as:

- can inspection be beneficial to schools?
- how can assessment procedures help pupils learn?
- how can school self-evaluation improve teaching and learning?
- what impact does leadership in the school have in the classroom?
- how can school improvement become classroom improvement?

The books are grounded in sound theory, recent research evidence and best practice, and aim to:

- help you to make meaning personally and professionally from knowledge in a given field;
- help you to seek out practical applications of an area of knowledge for classrooms and schools;
- help those of you who want to research the field in greater depth, by providing key sources with accessible summaries and recommendations.

In addition, each chapter ends with a series of questions for reflection or further discussion, enabling schools to use the books as a resource for whole-school staff development.

We hope that the books in this series will show you that there are ways of raising achievement that can take account of how schools grow and develop and how teachers work and interact with one another. *What's in it for schools?* – a great deal, we think!

Introduction to this book

James Learmonth's credentials for writing this book include his experience of being on the receiving end of the inspection process as a teacher and a head-teacher in the Inner London Education Authority; subsequently as one of Her Majesty's Inspectors (HMI); then as a Chief Inspector in a Local Education Authority and an OFSTED Registered Inspector. His Scottish ancestry and his international experience have constantly reminded him that the English way of doing things is not the only way and certainly not necessarily the best way.

In this book the author reminds us how and why inspections were first introduced – what *was* in it for schools? He briefly describes how the inspection system developed in England over the last hundred or so years and then discusses the current system, of which he has some criticisms. James Learmonth passionately believes that inspection can be beneficial to schools and describes how inspections could be linked to school self-evaluation and school improvement. In the final chapter, drawing on evidence from other countries, he argues that external inspection should support schools in their efforts to raise standards and that self-evaluation should play a greater part in the process. School inspectors, he says, can still have a unique role in 'affording assistance' (as Sir James Kay-Shuttleworth instructed his inspectors in 1840), and when conducted with rigour and integrity school inspections can be constructive, productive and contribute to school improvement.

Kate Myers and John MacBeath
June 2000

Acknowledgements

The great joy of being a school inspector is that you learn everywhere you go. I have learnt much from every group in the education community, including school pupils, and the ideas and approach included in this book have emerged from conversations, observations and other types of work over many years. But it's one thing to talk and observe, another to write: it's a daunting task producing a book about school inspection, because Matthew Arnold raised most of the really interesting issues during the first fifty years of the inspectorate's history. But I am very grateful to Kate Myers and John MacBeath, the Series Editors, for giving me this opportunity.

There are, I believe, some fresh and constructive ideas about inspection in this book, and I'm not sure if I can claim credit for any of them. Amongst those whose ideas, values and practice may or may not be accurately reflected are George Alexander, John Bangs, Alan Bassett, Cary Bazalgette, Roger Booker, Margaret Caistor, Simon Clements, Kim Day, Carol Donoughue, Norma Empringham, Lynne Gerlach, David Green, Manford Holmes, Jim Honeybone, Maggie Hughes, Elizabeth Jones, Andrew Macalpine, John MacBeath, Colin McCall, Alasdair Macdonald, Peter Mortimore, Anne Mountfield, Kate Myers, Chris Power, Jane Reed, Rick Richards, Rony Robinson, David Rowles, Mollie Sayer, Edwin Scott, Diana Shulla, John Singh, David Soulsby, Louise Stoll, Hazel Taylor, Roger Williams, Tom Wilson and Tom Wylie. In different ways, Sheila Browne and Eric Bolton were marvellous mentors to have.

I am grateful for their support and encouragement to all my colleagues in the Centre for Education Leadership and School

Improvement (CELSI), Canterbury Christ Church University College.

Angela Barker, Alun Davies, Maggie Hughes, Anna Learmonth, Rebecca Learmonth and Nicola Wright were of immense help in preparing the text, and the comments of the Series Editors and Anna Clarkson at Falmer were both supportive and challenging – a balance we will hear more about later in the book.

Thanks to the following for permission to reproduce illustrative material: Mary Evans Picture Library for the cartoons on pages 50 and 68; Atlantic Syndication for extracts from the *Daily Mail* (p. 55), *Evening Standard* (p. 9), and *Metro* (p. 73); News International Syndication for the extract from *The Sun* (p. 52); *The Daily Telegraph* for extracts on pages 12 and 32; *Scotland on Sunday* for the extract on page 61; *The Times Educational Supplement* for extracts on pages 7, 18, 39, and 104; the *Daily Express* for the extract on page 117; *The Observer* for extracts on pages 62 and 76; *The Guardian* for extracts on page 7; Punch Ltd. for the cartoons on pages vi and 25; Neil Dishington for the cartoons on pages 45 and 139; John Morland for the cartoon on page 12; Bill Stott for the cartoons on pages 49 and 108; Martin Rowson and the *TES* for the cartoon on page 19; Priestley and *The Independent* for the cartoon on page 59 and the extract on page 21; Bob Bibby and Pierrepoint Press for the extract from *Be a Falling Leaf* (ISBN 0 9533196 0 1); Manchester University Press for the extract from *A Ragged Schooling* by Robert Roberts; Gervase Phinn and Penguin UK for the extract from *The Other Side of the Dale*.

1 Introduction

For several years the reports on this school have been uniformly favourable. The last two reports were very detailed. It is not easy to say anything in praise of the work which has not already been said; and no criticism is either necessary or possible. All the work of the school continues to be not only excellent of its kind but unusually varied and advanced. When a Head Master of the professional skill and versatility of Mr Learmonth gathers round him a highly competent staff, minute reports become superfluous.

(HM Inspector's Report on Girthon Public School,
Gatehouse-of-Fleet, 1902)

No twenty-first century school inspector would get away with this report, which HMI Francis Jamieson wrote in 1902 of the school where my grandfather was head-master for over thirty years. But as the purposes and processes of inspection have varied over nearly two centuries, one central tension has remained constant: to what extent is school inspection about helping schools to improve? And to what extent is school inspection a process of accountability, whereby society requires those working in schools to justify the quality of education they provide and the efficiency with which they use public money?

In this book, I explore this tension from the perspectives of three partners: central government, local government and the individual school. It will become clear that I believe in inspection both as a tool for accountability and as a powerful force for school improvement. If I have major reservations about OFSTED's profile and procedures, I also recognise the responsibility to suggest something different which will fulfil these two functions more effectively.

In Chapter 2, I describe some of the main elements in current debates about inspection, offer some interpretation of evidence about the impact of OFSTED inspection on schools, and raise some questions about the role of Her Majesty's Chief Inspector of Schools (HMCI). The roles of central government, of the Local Education Authority (LEA), of the individual school and of other stakeholders are explored in Chapter 3: where were their roots and how have they grown? Chapter 4 explores the part inspection plays in the circumstances of schools in difficulty: should the school community itself always bear the brunt of a very critical inspection report? What kind of inspection would help these schools to improve their standards? Chapter 5 draws on international research and other evidence about the processes of school improvement, and their relationship with inspection. In Chapter 6, I try to bring together the most positive elements from UK and international experience of school evaluation and outline a combination of internal self-review and external inspection which will help schools in their quest to raise levels of student achievement in the twenty-first century. I try to reflect on what's in it for schools in the Conclusion.

During the last twenty years I have been fortunate to work as an inspector in a variety of roles: as an HMI during the 1980s, as Chief Inspector in an LEA in the early 1990s, and as an OFSTED Registered Inspector in the mid-1990s. I have watched, always with interest and occasionally with delight or horror, the radical changes which have taken place. One welcome change is that the purposes and procedures of inspection are now explicit and accessible to public scrutiny and debate. Many of these debates have been played out in the media, which are not only important vehicles for the discussion of issues of public concern, but also significant influences on the shaping of the discourse. Many educators have been slow to accept the contribution which the media can make to increasing the public understanding of educational issues; perhaps they have had bad experiences of the media in the past, or believe the media are only interested in 'bad news'. In order to increase the constituency of interest and support for education, and to include school inspection as one of the issues which should be open to public debate, we need the media. It would be foolish to ignore the contribution the media make, or to omit examples of how the media represent the issues. So the text is complemented by extracts from the press, and by relevant cartoons.

Issues about how schools can best use inspection are complex and diverse. My purpose is not to offer practical tips to the school awaiting inspection, but to explore how an external system of school evaluation can complement internal self-evaluation in ways that both promote school improvement and satisfy demands for accountability. I am conscious that a book of this length, and with this purpose, can only touch upon important and interesting secondary aspects of school inspection. Where possible, I have tried to include 'a taster' of these issues, or at least included a reference which may be followed up by an interested reader.

Just as the purposes and processes of school inspection have changed over time, so has the role of the inspector. What is missing in some current perceptions of an OFSTED inspector (though not in many real-life individuals) is a sense of partnership with school-teachers, of mutual respect, of joint journeying and learning in order to serve better the interests of school pupils. The previous HMCI (Her Majesty's Chief Inspector), Chris Woodhead, has commented on what he calls the 'demonisation' of school inspectors by teachers' organisations and others. It is important to represent inspectors as normal human beings, with typical strengths and weaknesses. I have therefore also included a range of perspectives on school inspectors from fiction and other literary sources. Inspectors should, in the wonderful phrase used about the first national school inspectors, 'afford assistance', and they should do so with both courage and modesty. I hope, too, that some of the enjoyment of inspecting, and learning as you go, is evident in the text.

On a visit to a New York elementary school in 1988, I joined a class of nine-year-olds who had been working for three weeks on a project about 'Famous People'. I stopped at the desk of a girl who appeared to have written only three sentences about her chosen famous person, Socrates. I was about to chide her for not writing more about so famous and attractive a figure when I remembered my training as an inspector: I should study the evidence.

'Socrates was a wise old man. He gave people advice. They poisoned him.'

I moved quietly on to the next desk.

2 The context of school inspection

This introductory chapter sets the process of inspection in its contemporary context, describes some of the evidence related to its strengths and weaknesses, and briefly explores issues about the current role of Her Majesty's Chief Inspector of Schools.

> *There should be with respect to education a vigilant eye everywhere; and many schools have, for want of that, sunk very materially indeed. Schools cannot be too much inspected and examined; and in the proportion as the respectable people in the neighbourhood look after them or neglect them, in that proportion, generally speaking, they either flourish or decay. Such an inspection of all schools throughout the kingdom, I think, would be an unspeakable blessing to society, and would be the means of conveying improvement, and suggesting information to teachers, and stirring them up and leading them to increase their efforts.*

> (Witness giving evidence to the Parliamentary Committee on the State of Education, 1834)

Few people working in education would argue at the beginning of the twenty-first century for an education system which does not include some process of school inspection. Citizens should know what is going on in their schools, and are entitled to some sort of account, quantitative and qualitative, of how money is invested and spent in the education system and of how schools are performing. If the current Government's priorities are 'education, education and education', then teachers as members of an important public service should seek as much information as possible about schools' performance so that they can reflect on their own and colleagues' practice, and make considered professional judgements about maintenance, development or innovation. A government too, is more likely to make informed and coherent decisions about educational policy if it has access to a substantial body of reliable and up-to-date information about schools' work and students' performance. Finally, we have a responsibility to provide all children with the best possible education, and inspection is an important source of information about how successfully this aim is being achieved.

What sort of inspection?

But it's one thing for a society to agree the *need* for a system of school inspection, quite another for it to reach consensus on what *form* it should take. The primary purpose of school inspection will in large part determine the form of the process. I believe that the current process of inspection in England and Wales, introduced by the Education (Schools) Act 1992 which set up the Office for Standards in Education (OFSTED), had its roots in the Parent's Charter of 1991. The charter pledged access for parents to open inspection reports on all schools, so that their choice of school could be informed by clear, up-to-date information. The government of the day believed that standards in schools would be raised by parents using their choices in an open market: if schools were to continue to attract pupils, they would have to raise their standards in the face of local competition. All state schools were to be inspected within a four-year cycle, and inspectors would use a common and explicit 'framework' of criteria in making their judgements. The process of inspection, then, would create a situation whereby parents would, through their choices, drive up standards in schools.

The publication of school inspection reports, which started in 1983, has meant that the public, including educators, now have the opportunity to debate how such reports are compiled, whether or not they are likely to be a fair and accurate picture of how schools are working, and how the performance of schools may be improved. In addition to the continuing debate among professional educators, some commentators outside the education profession (e.g. Melanie Phillips 1996) have seen the debate in polarised terms: Chris Woodhead, the then HMCI, with a few allies including Melanie Phillips, represented the interests of children and par-

TES 2 February 1996

Largest private contractor lambasts OFSTED work

Inspection system 'fails in key areas'

by Nicholas Pyke

Guardian 2 June 1996

Consultants paid to prepare for Ofsted visits

Schools 'buy' good inspection reports

Donald Macleod
Education Correspondent

ents versus 'the education establishment', which was presented as reactionary, defensive and driven by self-interest. On the other hand, Francis Beckett (1999) argued that hopes of a better education service, with motivated, high quality and confident teachers, were doomed as long as the then HMCI, Chris Woodhead, remained in the post.

If the desirability of a school inspection system is granted, the next questions are to do with whether the present system is reliable, fair and effective. OFSTED has not been keen to debate the reliability or validity of its methodology, particularly conclusions based on inspectors' judgements. It has often preferred to cite high levels of head-teachers' satisfaction with the overall process, or the fact that 96 per cent of schools inspected in 1996/7 agreed that the then current Framework and Handbooks provided schools with a good basis for internal evaluation (OFSTED 1998c).

What does research tell us about OFSTED?

Commenting that the current OFSTED arrangements are both an embarrassment to anyone who understands social science and a source of grave distress to the teaching profession, and noting that there does not seem to have been a single published study of 'inter-rater reliability' from OFSTED, Fitz-Gibbon and Stephenson-Forster (1999) argue that OFSTED's methods have:

- been amateurish and far from 'state of the art' in that they have failed to meet even the most elementary standards with regard to sampling, reliability and validity;
- failed to implement the organisation's own principles, such as separating advice from inspection;
- failed to keep abreast of modern approaches to management and to research evidence;
- demanded analysis skills from inspectors without having demonstrated that inspectors have these skills to a degree which gives them authority in the interpretation of complex data and research evidence;
- confused its mission with that of other bodies;
- included methods which have now been quietly repudiated by OFSTED itself, but without apology or compensation made to the schools damaged by those methods now admitted to be indefensible.

(p. 115)

There have been many other attempts by academic professionals in the field and others to point out the strengths and weaknesses in the present OFSTED system. Scanlon (1999) recently asked heads and classroom teachers who had experienced an OFSTED inspection for their views:

The interview and survey data indicated that teachers were not opposed to school inspection as such, and believed that account-ability in education was essential. They objected to the OFSTED model of inspection because it seemed to create as many problems as it solved.

(p. 83)

Scanlon's data also suggest that head-teachers are consistently more positive than teaching staff about OFSTED inspection. Those who had experienced both OFSTED inspections and related HMI inspections found the latter more constructive, as HMI were seen as 'critical friends' (p. 81). She found a particularly worrying feature in schools which had been judged to require special measures:

The contrast between declining staff morale and improvements in standards in education was one of the main findings of the research; there would appear to be an inverse relationship between the two variables. Whilst acknowledging that improve-ments had been made, most of those interviewed felt that there

Evening Standard 9 June 1998

FARCE OF THE SCHOOL REPORTS

Same primary gets black marks and gold stars from different inspectors

THE reliability of education watchdog Ofsted was thrown into doubt today.

by JOEL WOLCHOVER
Education Correspondent

were better and more effective ways of achieving the same ends. They recognised that changes were necessary at their schools, but felt that the level of stress and 'public humiliation' generated by the process was unnecessary and even counter-productive. It was felt that whilst the special measures process had addressed some problems, it had also created new problems or aggravated existing ones.

(p. 83)

Despite the evidence presented to it by academics and the professional associations, the recent House of Commons Education and Employment Committee (1999) appeared unconvinced by arguments of suspect methodology and concentrated on 'the scale of administrative error in relation to some lesson observations', a charge which OFSTED was able easily to absorb: 'OFSTED will be looking carefully at means of ensuring that this poor practice does not occur.' (House of Commons Education and Employment Committee 1999b)

Fitz-Gibbon and Stephenson-Forster (1999) are also concerned about fairness, in particular the fact that the OFSTED ratings of schools appears to deliver ratings which are worse for schools in the most difficult circumstances. They acknowledge that this is not a recent phenomenon, and that pre-OFSTED inspections were open to the same criticism. (Gray and Hannon 1986)

Three other major studies of OFSTED have been recently reported:

(a) *The OFSTED System of School Inspection: An Independent Evaluation* (Brunel University, 1999)
(b) *The Work of OFSTED* (House of Commons Education and Employment Committee 1999a)
(c) *Improving Schools and Inspection: the Self-Inspecting School* (Ferguson *et al.* 2000)

Summaries of (a) and (b) are included in the Appendix.

In very general terms, several consistent conclusions emerge from all three studies and are set out below:

- There is a clear consensus that the school system should continue to have a national system of inspection, and that there should be a regular cycle of inspection – though not all schools may need the same 'type' of inspection.
- OFSTED's 'Framework for the inspection of schools' was welcomed as an open and constructive set of criteria for the evaluation of schools.
- The system causes widespread disruption, and often considerable stress, to the normal routine of the school.
- There is a lack of confidence in the methodology of OFSTED's collection and analysis of evidence before, during and after inspection.
- The capacity of the school to use an OFSTED inspection constructively is strongly linked to the relationships developed between the particular team of OFSTED inspectors and the school community.
- There is little evidence that OFSTED inspection is an effective catalyst for school improvement in the pre-inspection period, or in the immediate post-inspection period.
- The feedback given to teachers rarely has much effect on their classroom practice.
- Inspection does not do enough to foster the growth of skills in self-evaluation.
- Judgements may be unreliable and yet have serious consequences for individuals.
- Granted the time, money and personnel involved, an OFSTED inspection gives too little attention to constructive advice (not prescription) about future development, to the 'how' of school improvement.
- It is difficult to find clear evidence that the OFSTED system gives value for money in fulfilling what was said (1998) to be its main purpose.

For further, and predominately critical, evidence about OFSTED's inspection methodology, see Cedric Cullingford's (1999) collection of studies.

Daily Telegraph 6 July 1994

How to waste £112 million

John Clare explains how school inspection, the key to the Parent's Charter, has become an expensive farce

Same suit. Same lesson notes.
Now for a repeat performance of 1963.

But school inspection has never operated, or been expected to operate, on a social scientific basis. Inspectors have won (or lost) their respect and credibility through what has been referred to as a 'connoisseur' role – the idea that a skilled and widely-experienced practitioner is the best person to make judgements about the quality of a school's provision and to advise schools (if this is legitimate) on a range of possible approaches to school improvement. In the twenty-first century an approach to inspection which does not take into account the sophisticated methods of collecting and analysing data which are now available is unlikely to command wide respect. Yet there are other strong arguments which suggest that the subtle processes of teaching and learning, and of the management of school improvement, are undermined and trivialised if quantitative methods only are used in making judgements. If qualitative methods are included, as I believe they should be, then the skills and expertise of experienced practitioners are vital elements in evaluating the quality of educational provision. 'Connoisseurs' in the fast-moving world of education are entitled to further training, and to regular opportunities to meet and debate issues of professional concern with colleagues from a diverse range of professional backgrounds. Neither of these opportunities is widely available to OFSTED inspectors at the moment.

The notion of school evaluation by 'connoisseurs' is particularly associated with Elliot Eisner (1985) who argues for artistry in both teaching itself and in the evaluation of the educational process.

> I do not believe that education as a process, or schooling as an institution designed to foster that process, or teaching as an activity that most directly mediates that process is likely to be controlled by a set of laws that can be transformed into a prescription or recipe for teaching. I do not believe we will ever have a 'Betty Crocker' theory of education. Teaching is an activity that requires artistry, schooling itself is a cultural artefact, and education is a process whose features may differ from individual to individual, context to context. Therefore what I believe we need to do with respect to educational evaluation is not to seek recipes to control and measure practice, but rather to enhance whatever artistry the teacher can achieve. Theory plays a role in the cultivation of artistry, but its role is not prescriptive, it is diagnostic. Good theory in education, as in art, helps us see more.
>
> (p. 91)

Writing from the other side of the world, and long before OFSTED came into being, Eisner has great sympathy with the restlessness and, sometimes, hostility which teachers have towards an evaluation system which they see as mechanical and top-down:

> The pressures toward accountability defined in terms of specific operational objectives and precise measurement of outcomes are pressures that many teachers dislike. Their distaste for these pressures is not due to professional laziness, recalcitrance, or stupidity, but is due to the uneasy feeling that as rational as a means–ends concept of accountability appears to be, it doesn't quite fit the educational facts with which they live and work. Many teachers, if you ask them, are unable to state why they feel uneasy. They have a difficult time articulating what the flaws are in the often glib prescriptions that issue from state capitols and from major universities. Yet the uneasiness is often – not always but often – justified. Some objectives one cannot articulate, some goals one does not achieve by the end of the academic year, some insights are not measurable, some ends are not known until after the fact, some models of educational practice violate some visions of the learner and the classroom. Many teachers have developed sufficient connoisseurship to feel that something is awry but have insufficient connoisseurship to provide a more adequate conceptualisation of just what it is.
>
> (p. 110)

OFSTED and the education system

Not all of the recent changes have had an obvious and immediate impact upon the individual school. Until the early 1990s, there was a national structure for Her Majesty's Inspectorate of Schools in England and Wales, with teams of inspectors who covered both subjects and regions. Subject and phase committees met regularly to exchange and analyse evidence about the strength and weakness of provision, and each 'district' (normally an LEA) had a team of inspectors who provided a continuing link between schools (and further education) and the Department of Education and Science (DES), as it then was. Changes introduced by the Education (Schools) Act of 1992 split the inspection service (OFSTED, as it became) from the Department of Education and Science and introduced a system of inspection based on freelance inspectors working on the basis of a competitive tender and contract for each school. In addition to the issues arising from the inspection of individual schools by freelance inspectors, there are many other relevant issues which are not dealt with in detail in this book. These include issues about whether Government policy in education has suffered from the removal of a schools' inspectorate which was more directly involved in the formation of education policy, and which was out 'in the field' and able to report back to the DfEE about the effects of that policy. For a clear and powerful account of these changes, and an explanation of why the present arrangements may be a source of anxiety, see the reflections of a previous Senior Chief Inspector, Eric Bolton (Bolton 1998).

One of the mysteries not covered in Bolton's account is how the same Conservative government, led first by Margaret Thatcher and then by John Major, tolerated in Scotland a process of school inspection very different from that introduced in England and Wales. Much of the argument in this book is based on the situation in England and Wales, though in my view the current Scottish system has much to commend it. Many of the elements in the present Scottish system will be reflected in Chapter 6, which looks forward to a system of school inspection which promotes school improvement so that standards may be further raised.

In general, there is a strong case to be made for HMI as a professional 'arm' of central government. As Lawton and Gordon (1987) point out, one of the problems with education is that many people, having been to school themselves, believe themselves to be experts on the subject. Civil servants and politicians are often tempted to express their views on, or interfere in, educational matters in a much less restrained way than they would in matters of medical or technical expertise.

OFSTED and LEAs

This book is concerned primarily with the relationship between inspection and schools. But one of the most significant educational developments within the last few years has been OFSTED's inspection of LEAs. The purpose of these inspections has been to review the way LEAs perform their functions and, in particular, to determine the contributions which LEA support, including support to individual pupils, makes to school improvement. Both the methodology of these inspections and the capacity of school inspectors to make sound judgements about LEA processes of which they may have little or no experience have been questioned (e.g. Kogan 1996). It is also true that the OFSTED verdict on LEAs has in many cases provoked considerable controversy (e.g. Birmingham, Calderdale, Islington, Liverpool, Manchester and Tower Hamlets – all LEAs with at least a core of urban, socially disadvantaged territory). This is not the right place to develop the debate about OFSTED's inspections of LEAs, but it would be naive to suppose that a highly critical and negative verdict on an LEA does not have repercussions on the schools within that LEA.

Drawing conclusions from inspections of the first forty-four LEAs, OFSTED (2000c) has begun to sketch its image of the effective LEA:

> First, well-run LEAs have clear and minimalist definitions of monitoring, challenge, intervention and support, which are reflected in the targeting of their resources. They retain no more funding than is strictly necessary to fulfil their statutory responsibilities. As a result, they are high delegaters, not only of funding, but of real autonomy. They ask themselves rigorously questions such as:
>
> > 'do we need to do this?'
> > 'can someone else do it better?'
> > 'can it be done more cheaply?'
>
> They have no ideological predilection either for the public or the private sector. They consult well with stakeholders, and enjoy the trust of their schools. They understand well the implications of multi-agency working, and are able to manage them at the operational as well as the strategic level. Finally, they have a strategy for and the ability to enhance the school's own capacity to sustain improvement.
>
> (pp. 2–3)

The role of HMCI

Eric Bolton (1998), a former Senior Chief Inspector, argues that the independence conferred on the HMCI has created a post that is 'out of control'. Chris Woodhead, Bolton believes, openly chose to be polemical, and to express his views on important matters.

> The problem is that it is not clear, and cannot be clear, in present circumstances, when the HMCI is expressing his own opinions, and when he is voicing a collective judgement based on the findings of wide-ranging inspection. It is important to decide under which, if any, circumstances the personal views of an HMCI are of value, and if it is possible for an HMCI to be credible and widely influential if it is known that at times he might choose to be polemical.
>
> (p. 54)

Robin Alexander (1999) – with Chris Woodhead and Jim Rose one of the 'three wise men' in an influential DES discussion paper on primary education (1992) – provides an example of an occasion when HMCI's views seem categorically opposed to inspection evidence. From the autumn of 1997 onwards, and in a variety of speeches, press releases and letters, the then HMCI made clear his view, which he claimed was based on inspection evidence, that the Government would not be able to meet its targets on improved literacy and numeracy unless the non-core elements of the curriculum were drastically slimmed down. His views played a significant part in polarising the debate between 'curriculum breadth' and improved 'standards in the basics'. Yet OFSTED (1997b) published a report on its statistical analysis of the relationship between inspection data and national test results at Key Stage 2:

> The main finding was that schools which did well in the tests (in English, Mathematics and Science at Key Stage 2) also provide a broad and balanced curriculum. On average, schools awarded a high grade for curriculum balance and breadth score well in the tests and those awarded lower grades score less well. This trend persists across all schools analysed regardless of their context.
>
> (OFSTED 1997b, para 3)

It was not only OFSTED's own evidence of inspection that HMCI seemed content to ignore. He made clear on a number of occasions his strong views that much educational research is of poor quality and of

TES 18 December 1998

Tests are unreliable says chief inspector

By **Sarah Cassidy**

little use to teachers or others within the education system. OFSTED's commissioned study of educational research (Tooley and Darby 1998) concluded that considerable sums of money were being pumped into research of dubious quality and of little value, and that the crucial areas of initial teacher education and in-service training are being ill-served by the research community. Granted that OFSTED commissions and uses research findings, Chris Woodhead may be open to the charge that he chose to accept research evidence which supported his predetermined viewpoint, or which were comfortably aligned with political priorities.

In response to similar comments made in the House of Commons Education and Employment Committee's Report (1999b), OFSTED has commented:

> We are aware that many of the witnesses invited by the Committee to give evidence commented on the style adopted by HMCI. The Committee did, of course, for the most part, choose to interview known critics of OFSTED and HMCI. Neither did the Committee take into account the views of parents and the wider public. It is, in our view, vital that the Chief Inspector continues to report clearly on the strengths and weaknesses of the education system. We reject the assertion that some of Mr Woodhead's views cannot be sub-stantiated by inspection or other evidence. They can.
>
> (1997b, para. 47)

The implication of these remarks is that Chris Woodhead believed that he spoke for the interests of parents, children and 'the wider public', if necessary in the face of protests from the majority of professionals involved in education. Woodhead's assumption of advocacy on behalf of non-professionals is key to the understanding of his involvement in the media – though OFSTED also regrets 'the tendency of the media's coverage of education to highlight controversy and to focus on failure'.

So how does Chris Woodhead see the role of OFSTED's HMCI? His Annual Lectures (1995–9) provide some interesting evidence. For example, on the topic of 'the reflective practitioner' he will avoid the 'easy comforts of polemic':

> It is (OFSTED's) job, standing independent of both political imperatives and educational orthodoxies, to comment on what is happening and to ask the right questions at the right time.

He sees his role as influencing the 'professional culture' of teachers so that it is:

TES 18 June 1999

less resistant to change . . . less eager to take refuge in simplistic and untenable dichotomies . . . if we can only jettison the pretension and pomposity and empty romanticism of 'reflective practice' for the practical realities of 'tinkering', then we might stand a chance of moving forward in the right direction . . . put bluntly, do we want 'reflective practitioners' or teachers who can teach children to read?
(Woodhead 1998)

It is hard to imagine what evidence OFSTED might have from school inspection about the classroom effectiveness of 'reflective practitioners', let alone whether they conform with his 'simplistic and untenable dichotomy' between reflective practitioners or teachers who can teach children to read. It is clear from this and other examples that Chris Woodhead saw the role of HMCI as taking up provocative positions within the professional debate, and within wider lay conversations.

Another type of inspection?

Referring to Chris Woodhead's oft-quoted remark that all he needed was one day in a school to form judgements about its quality, John MacBeath and Kate Myers (1999) accept that some schools feel more 'comfortable' to the visitor than others. But they go on to suggest a quite different form of inspection from that in which criteria for judgement are rigidly predetermined, and have within them clear assumptions about what constitutes an effective school, and what will cause school improvement:

the culture, rhythms and patterns of organisational life lie much more deeply buried. They are only discernible over time, and are never static enough to be pinned down with precision. That is why inspection works best and is most positively received when feedback is given not as something definitive and objective, but as an agenda for discussion. Inspection is most effective when it offers opportunities for school leaders and inspectors together to reflect critically and openly on these deep-lying, but highly significant, aspects of school quality.
(p. 121)

These remarks clearly envisage a quite different process of school inspection, one which will be developed in later chapters of the book.

QUESTIONS FOR FURTHER EXPLORATION

1 From your own experience, what are the strengths and weaknesses of the present OFSTED system of inspection?

2 Look back at the recent survey evidence on page 11. Which aspects of the evidence do you find particularly persuasive? Are there arguments presented there with which you disagree on the basis of your personal experience, or for other reasons?

3 What do you believe is the proper role for HMCI? Are you convinced by Chris Woodhead's view of the role as an advocate for parents and the wider public? How might it contribute to the raising of standards in schools?

4 What blend of 'scientific' and 'artistic' elements is likely to form the most effective basis for school inspection? What blend will most effectively help schools improve?

5 What role does the LEA currently play in supporting or challenging schools in your area? If it has been inspected by OFSTED, what were the effects on schools? What are the LEA's strengths and weaknesses in relation to school improvement?

Independent 6 January 1999

Ofsted chief hits back at 'demonisers'

BY BEN RUSSELL
AND JUDITH JUDD

THE CHIEF Inspector of Schools attacked his critics yesterday, saying union leaders and academics were damaging the reputation of teachers by "demonising" inspectors.

3 How did the inspection process develop?

This chapter outlines the development of the part played by different agencies in the evaluation of schools in England: central government, the Local Education Authority (LEA), the individual school, including stakeholders, teachers, governors, school students and parents.

> *If the scholarship of some of the older generation of inspectors was waterlogged, their bodies in some cases suffered under the weight of quite other liquids. The inspectors were usually entertained to lunch, sometimes by the headmaster, sometimes by a local patron. An inspector, lunching with a farmer, related that he had asked a boy that morning who had written 'Hamlet' and the boy had tremblingly replied, 'Please, Sir, it wisna me!' The farmer laughed heartily, adding, 'An' I suppose the wee devil had dune it a' the time.'*
>
> *It is related that an old headmaster, in another town, having enjoyed himself as well as the inspector, felt altogether too comfortable to work in the afternoon, or to think out a task for the pupils. So he sat down in his chair, told the children to take out their drawing books, and folding his arms, with his head drooping on his chest, muttered before lapsing into blissful unconsciousness, 'Draw me!'*

(Thomson 1936)

The role of central government

Tensions within the role of school inspector, and between inspectors and schools are not new. They have their roots deep in the history of inspection. Th̶e̶ ̶e̶a̶r̶liest schools were church schools, and church leaders during occasional visits to their schools reflected a 'visitorial tradition' which was one of partnership, or even 'the family'. The churches and religious societies used 'visitors' to establish new schools, to learn what was happening in existing schools, and to help improve them all. Andrew Bell, secretary of the National Society from 1812 to 1819, put forward one 'correct method of instruction' and employed visitors to ensure that teachers in the Society's schools were doing what they were supposed to be doing.

School inspectors as such were the product of the Industrial Revolution. The first were appointed in 1833 under the Factory Act to explore the establishment of schools for the children of those working in factories. National interest in the education of the large number of poor children increased, and in 1839 the Committee of the Privy Council on Education formally established Government inspection of schools with the appointment of two school inspectors. The Committee's first Secretary, Dr J. P. Kay (later Sir James Kay-Shuttleworth), issued important instructions to his new inspectors:

> It is of the utmost consequence that you should bear in mind that this inspection is not intended as a means of exercising control, but of affording assistance: that it is not to be regarded as operating for the restraint of local efforts, but for their encouragement; and that its chief objects will not be attained without the co-operation of the school committees; – the Inspector having no power to interfere, and not being instructed to offer advice or information excepting where it is invited.
>
> (Minutes of the Committee of Council on Education, 1840–41)

School improvement was at the heart of school inspection from the start, though how this might best be achieved and the most effective role of the inspector were open to debate. There were, of course, other purposes, the chief of which was to collect facts and information and report on them to the government of the day.

It soon became clear that the two inspectors were not equally acceptable in Church of England, non-conformist and Roman Catholic schools: accordingly, the structure of the inspectorate was to develop along denominational lines with separate inspectors for each group.

Matthew Arnold

Matthew Arnold, perhaps the best-known HMI of all, submitted an annual series of reports on his visits to non-conformist schools between 1852 and 1880. In them he sets out with clarity and insight almost all of the issues which are important in debates about the context, process and tone of school inspections.

There is an advantage in the same inspector, where it is possible, continuing to see the same school year after year; he acquires in this way a knowledge of it which he can never gain from a single visit, and he becomes acquainted not with the instruction and discipline only of the school, but also with its local circumstances and difficulties. These local circumstances and difficulties, it is of advantage, no doubt, that the inspector should know: it is a most important question, and one in necessity of a clear resolution of which becomes daily more and more apparent to me, in what manner and to what extent this knowledge should affect his report on a school to your Lordships. I constantly hear it urged that consideration for local difficulties and peculiar circumstances should induce him to withhold the notice of his report of shortcomings and failures, because these may have been caused by circumstances for which neither managers nor teachers were to blame, and because the statement of them may unfavourably affect a struggling school. There is some plausibility in this plea for silence; but it is based, I feel sure, on a misconception of what the peculiar province and duty of an Inspector is. The first duty is that of a simple and faithful report to your Lordships; the knowledge that imperfections in a school have been occasioned wholly or in part by peculiar local difficulties, may very properly restrain him from recommending the refusal of grants to that school; but it ought not to restrain him from recording the imperfections. But although I thus press for the most unvarnished and literal report on their schools, I can assure the teachers of them that it is far from no harshness or want of sympathy towards them that I do so. No one feels more than I do how laborious is their work, how trying at times to the health and spirits, how full of difficulty even for the best ... the quantity of work actually done by teachers is immense: the sincerity and devotedness of much of it is even affective. They themselves will be the greatest gainers by a system of reporting which clearly states what they do and what they fail to do: not one which drowns alike success and failure, the able and the inefficient in a common flood of vague approbation.

(Annual Report, 1854)

Who is likely to be of more help to a school in its efforts to improve, an inspector who knows the school or one who does not? What are the 'local circumstances and difficulties' which affect the performance of a school, and how should an inspector deal with them in making judgements about quality or in writing a report? Are 'unvarnished and literal' reports the most effective way of delivering judgements? What is the appropriate relationship between those inspecting and those being inspected? Arnold dealt with all these questions.

Punch 1900

A WISE CHILD.

Inspector. "SUPPOSE I LENT YOUR FATHER £100 IN JUNE, AND HE PROMISED TO PAY ME BACK £10 ON THE FIRST OF EVERY MONTH, HOW MUCH WOULD HE OWE ME AT THE END OF THE YEAR? NOW THINK WELL BEFORE YOU ANSWER."

Pupil. "£100, SIR."

Inspector. "YOU'RE A VERY IGNORANT LITTLE GIRL. YOU DON'T KNOW THE MOST ELEMENTARY RULES OF ARITHMETIC!"

Pupil. "AH, SIR, BUT YOU DON'T KNOW FATHER!"

Payment by results

By the middle of the nineteenth century, inspectors were finding it difficult to do their work without commenting on social conditions and criticising policies and authority. Robert Lowe, the then Secretary of Education, issued a Minute to all inspectors:

> Inspectors must confine themselves to the state of the schools under their inspection and to practical suggestions for their improvement. If any report in the judgement of their Lordships does not conform to the standard it is to be returned to the inspector for revision and if, on its being again received and it appears to be open to the same objection, it is to be put aside as a document not proper to be printed at the public expense.
>
> (1861)

The *Revised Code*, introduced by Robert Lowe in 1862, led to a very different role for HMI. Inspectors were to be the 'competent authority' who visited schools and tested students in reading, writing, arithmetic and (for girls) needlework. Test results, plus attendance figures, determined the size of each school's grant, and became the basis of 'payment by results'.

Matthew Arnold was appalled by the change in role for inspectors demanded by the *Revised Code*, and its implications for inspectors' relationship with schools. Under the old system:

> the prime aim and object of the inspector's visit was, after ensuring the fulfilment of certain sanitary and disciplinary conditions, to test and quicken the intellectual life of the school. The scholars and teachers co-operated, therefore, with the inspectors in doing their best to reach (this object); they were anxious for his judgement after he was gone. At present the centre of interest for the school when the inspector visits it is changed. Scholars and teachers have their thoughts directed straight upon the new examination, which will bring, they know, such important benefit to the school if it goes well and bring it such important loss if it goes ill.
>
> (Annual Report 1863)

With the initiative and flexibility removed from HMI's role and a much more 'mechanical' task imposed for each school visit, Arnold became even more disillusioned and foresaw consequences for inspectors' relationship with schools:

> The school examinations in view of payment by results are, as I have said, a game of 'mechanical contrivances' in which the teacher will and must more and more learn how to beat us.

It is important not to have too nostalgic a view of the old-style HMI. Dunford (1998) reminds us that in the nineteenth century schools were apprehensive about 'inspection day' because there was so much at stake for the managers and teachers, and that some HMI abused the power they had and appeared self-important and overbearing. In *Lark Rise to Candleford*, Flora Thompson (1945) offers a pupil's perspective on contemporary HMI:

> Her Majesty's Inspector of Schools came once a year on a date of which previous notice had been given. There was no singing or quarrelling on the way to school that morning. The children, in clean pinafores and well-blackened boots, walked deep in thought; or, with open spelling or table books in hand, tried to make up in an hour for all their wasted yesterdays. . . . Ten – eleven – the hands of the clock dragged on, and forty-odd hearts might be heard thumping when at last came the sound of wheels crunching on gravel and two top hats and the top of a whip appeared outside the upper panes of the large end window. Her Majesty's Inspector was an elderly clergyman, a little man with an immerse paunch and tiny grey eyes like gimlets. He had the reputation of being 'strict', but that was a mild way of describing his autocratic demeanour and scathing judgement. . . . What kind of man the inspector really was it is impossible to say. He may have been a great scholar, a good parish priest, and a good friend and neighbour to people of his own class. One thing, however, is certain, he did not care for or understand children.

> (p.9)

Inspectors and teachers

Payment by results petered out towards the end of the nineteenth century, and most HMIs and teachers in elementary schools were pleased. Because school grants were based on individual student test scores, the evaluation of teacher performance and of teacher pay became linked to how well the teacher's students performed for an inspector. Teachers became increasingly angry, and better organised: tensions with inspectors were frequent. In 1888 an HMI had decided that Frank Silverlock's parchment as a teacher should not be renewed because he had noted in a lesson observation that some boys had asked questions, thus displaying a lack of discipline. Two months later, when the management committee of the local board demanded his resignation, Frank Silverlock threw himself in front of a train at Highbury station, leaving a suicide note for his parents:

'I hope my act will be forgiven, and I shall go to where there are no dull stupid boys, and no inspectors.'

(Betts 1986: 18)

It often fell to heads to tell pupil-teachers whether or not they had been approved by a visiting inspector. My grandfather's school log for 1906 describes such a situation.

A newspaper for teachers, *The Schoolmaster*, commented on teachers' testimony to the Cross Commission, set up in 1888 to examine the state of elementary education:

The Inspectors of schools were the subject of many hard sayings, and the men, who under a system founded on common sense, would be deemed ornaments of the profession, are derided for their unfitness and irregularity. To be a university man is a good thing, but it by no means invariably implies the presence of a gentleman, and without long experience of the practical work of a teacher it as invariably implies a man unqualified for the work. . . . The pets of patronage have had their day.

(Betts 1986)

1906 211

7th Sept. On Monday morning of this week at half-past nine o'clock I informed Lizzie Campbell, pupil-teacher, that she had been unsuccessful in her examination – that at the end of the second year. She did her work in the usual manner all forenoon; and returned and did the afternoon's work also. She left school in company with Miss Kennedy and James McClellan about 20 minutes to five. At about five o'clock (p.m.) she left the house of her parents and has not since been seen by anyone. Diligent search has been made for her by bands of willing men and boys, but up to now without any success. Her tragic disappearance has cast a gloom not only upon the school, but upon the whole community.

13th Sept. Miss Campbell's body was got in the Canal last night.

Extract from W. Learmonth's school log

The Cross Commission subsequently recommended that well-quali-fied men with elementary school experience should be recruited to the Inspectorate. There was also to be tried the experiment of appointing women as 'sub-Inspectresses' to examine young children: Emily Jones had been appointed in 1883 as Directress of Needlework, the first woman HMI. The first ex-elementary school teacher was appointed in 1892, and two more women were appointed in 1895–6.

During the final years of the nineteenth century, as the government lost faith in 'Payment by results', a new freedom and trust in teachers was reflected in reports from the Committee of the Council on Education. HMI sought to regain teachers' respect, and in their negotiations with the newly-formed National Union of Teachers promised that HMI would never again judge the performance of an individual teacher, but would concentrate on the quality of teaching and learning in the school. However, the NUT was not to be quickly won over. In a submission to a Royal Commission on secondary education in 1894, the union pointed out that HM Inspectors lacked the qualities and experience of local school board inspectors, who they perceived to be generally helpful to the schools. Thus, the union argued, local boards, not HMI, should handle secondary school inspection.

In 1905, the Board of Education issued 'Suggestions for the consideration of teachers and others concerned with the work of Public Elementary Schools', which offered guidance to teachers and encouraged 'careful reflection on the practice of their profession'. However, no particular style of teaching and learning was advocated, let alone insisted upon:

> The only uniformity of practice that the Board of Education desire to see in the teaching of Public Elementary Schools is that each teacher shall think for himself, and work out himself such methods of teaching as may use his powers to the best advantage and be best suited to the particular needs and conditions of the school.
>
> (p. 6)

Expansion of the inspection service

Meanwhile, educational legislation enabled other sorts of school inspector to be appointed. The 1870 Forster Act created the new school boards which underpinned a national system of elementary schools, and they began to appoint their own inspectors. The 1902 Balfour Act abolished school boards and enabled the new Local Education Authorities (LEAs) to provide secondary education, and they too, began to appoint inspectors.

A new secondary branch of HMI was set up in 1903, and a new format for inspection emerged, involving a team of secondary inspectors who would visit for several days: the 'full inspection'.

> A school cannot be judged by a mere review of the subjects taught: it is a living thing: its life, which may have behind it a long tradition, extends beyond the classroom and must be grasped as a whole. Periodically, therefore, a comprehensive inspection of the school must be undertaken. The reason why a body of inspectors should undertake such an inspection is not so much that the skill of the specialist is needed to inspect specialists, but that collective judgement on all sides of school life and work is necessary. The inspectors do not make any claim to be either abler or better teachers or schoolmasters than many whom they meet in the course of their work, nor have any such claims ever been preferred on their behalf. So far as that aspect of things is concerned, they are no more than equals among equals.
>
> (Board of Education 1922–3)

The priorities of national inspection continued to swing, pendulum-like, between an inquisitorial and advising role until the 1950s, when HMI's profile was so low that questions were asked about its continued existence. However, in the late 1960s and 1970s HMI re-established an important national role in the increasingly heated debates about the state of public education: the Government sought to play a more active role, the performance of the LEAs came under increasing scrutiny, and educational issues of school organisation became more and more politicised. HMI seldom presented itself as an advocate for a particular position in the 'great debate' following James Callaghan's 1976 Ruskin College speech, but concentrated on providing a body of high-quality evidence about standards and the work of schools which could inform the debate. However, HMI did play a large part in the original thinking which informed the development of the National Curriculum, believing it would bring both greater rigour and consistency to the nation's schools.

Daily Telegraph 9 December 1991

How H.M Ideologues have laid waste school education

The progressive educational theories of HMI
have done lasting damage to schoolchildren
and a further reduction in its power should
be welcomed, says SHEILA LAWLOR

Opening up the inspection process

After Sir Keith Joseph, then Secretary of State, had instigated a thorough review of the current practice of HMI in 1982, the Rayner Report (DES 1983) set out the role of HMI in terms which reflected very closely the instructions issued to the first HMI about 140 years earlier:

> to assess standards and trends throughout the education system and to advise central Government on the state of the system nationally on the basis of its independent professional judgement. This is the first and overriding duty; and at the same time to contribute to the maintenance and improvement of standards in the system by the identification and dissemination of good practice; by bringing to notice weaknesses which require attention; and by advice to those with a direct responsibility for the operation of the service including teachers, heads and principals, governing bodies and local education authorities.

Sir Keith Joseph's decision in 1983 to publish all HMI reports raised the profile of HMI and inspection generally. The format and processes of school inspection came more to the public's attention, and publication provided early evidence of the use which could be made of an inspection report, positive or negative.

At the same time HMI were coming under attack from the Conservative Government and other Tory politicians. Despite the favourable report of Sir Derek Rayner in 1983, the Education Reform Act of 1988 gave LEAs new responsibilities in the monitoring and evaluation of the National Curriculum. But Tory politicians were not reassured. Both HMI and LEAs were, they claimed, at the mercy of 'educationalists':

> Here 'Educationalists' – frequently men and women of little classroom experience – nevertheless hold positions of considerable influence and power at senior DES levels, LEAs, Colleges of Education, and Post Graduate Teacher Training Courses. It is important that the Government finds a means of curbing the powers of these self-styled educationalists, who are often ardent advocates of Plowden-style education. From this position they:
>
> • exert considerable power over teaching advisors, local and HMI inspectors;
> • are allowed, unchecked, to improvise and introduce new (and unproven) teaching theories and methods into schools;
> • are in a position to dictate teaching practice to those teachers who have chosen to remain in the classroom throughout their careers instead of 'seeking promotion' on the educationalists' ladder;
> • all too frequently judge the promotion suitability of teachers not by their classroom skills and abilities or results, but through their fluency with the more fashionable educational theories of the day.
>
> (Carlton Club Political Committee 1991)

The performance of LEAs in developing inspection arrangements was judged in 1992 to have been 'too slow and uneven' and the Government could not let this continue. There would be an entirely new system of national inspection from 1992, featuring inspectors whom the Secretary of State, John Patten, referred to as 'big cats prowling on the educational landscape'. They would provide information on all schools, fulfilling the pledge in John Major's 'Citizen's Charter'.

John Patten's colourful language was enthusiastically inherited by Chris Woodhead, OFSTED's second HMCI appointed in 1993. His predecessor, Stewart Sutherland, had sustained the HMI tradition of basing his public utterances on interpretation of inspection evidence. Woodhead had no such inhibitions, and involved himself in the polemic of educational debate from the outset.

Central government and LEAs

Many of the school boards set up by the 1970 Education Act appointed inspectors, as did the LEAs which replaced school boards in 1902. Relationships with HMI were from the beginning uneasy, and were rooted in perceived differences in the qualifications of the different inspectorates. Tracing the history of LEA inspectorates, Birchenough (1946) is clear about the distinctions:

> The first local inspectors were appointed by the larger school boards. They were naturally men of altogether different antecedents and training from the traditional HMI Inspector. They had to be the eyes and ears of the school boards, but their primary function was to organise schools, report on them and secure a high standard of efficiency, for the payment of grant depended upon it. They were usually selected for successful elementary school experience. Their lot was cast in a mechanical age, an age which worshipped uniformity, when in educational circles the doctrine of formal training with all its implications remain unchallenged. Naturally some took their character from it. Because of this lack of imagination and inflexibility, they built an unpleasant reputation that lived on and did a disservice to local inspection . . . [in 1910] of 123 local inspectors of elementary schools, 109 men and 14 women, 104 were ex-elementary school teachers. Of the rest not more than two or three had the antecedents usually looked for by the Board of Education in the appointment of junior inspectors, that is to say, an education at a public school and then at Oxford or Cambridge. . . . As for the chief inspectors, they were the fountain heads of vicious officialdom. Only by replacing them by men of real culture and enlightenment was there any hope of educational problems being handled with freshness and originality if local inspection was to be continued.

LEA inspectorates

Some LEAs shied away from the title 'inspector', and appointed 'advisers' or 'organisers'. Very few LEAs carried out regular inspections of schools in their area before the mid-1980s, when the 1988 Education Reform Act encouraged LEAs to develop their capacity to inspect:

> The local inspectorates will need to monitor and evaluate school performance. They will need to provide LEAs and the schools themselves with trusted and informed professional advice, based on first-hand observation of what schools are actually doing, of the way in which they are implementing the National Curriculum, and of the standards achieved.
>
> (Baker 1988)

Reviewing progress made by LEAs in setting up systematic processes of monitoring and evaluation, Wilcox *et al.* (1993) found that there had been a significant increase in the amount of school evaluation undertaken by the majority of LEAs, and that many LEAs were involving school staff in various aspects of the inspection process. The line between those carrying out inspections and those being inspected was becoming blurred. Many LEAs were following up inspections with advice and many were holding discussions with the head or staff to review progress on implementing the inspector's recommendations. By 1993, almost three-fifths of LEAs in an NFER study had a rolling programme of full inspections; two-fifths did not carry out full inspections unless they were concerned about a particular school. However, even in LEAs which had a programme of full inspections, only a small number of schools were inspected each year. Median percentages of schools inspected in the academic year 1991/2 were 12 per cent of primary schools, 16 per cent of secondary schools and 14 per cent of special schools. These figures suggest that, on average, each school would have a full inspection every six to eight years (Maychell and Keys 1993). When asked in the study what was the most useful aspect of their school's most recent full inspection, heads frequently commented on their satisfaction that the inspection had provided reassurance that the school was 'on course'. Other elements that were commonly mentioned were the positive atmosphere which the inspection team had created, the objectivity and impartiality of the team, the opportunity to engage in future planning and the useful advice, information and ideas given by inspectors. The authors concluded that if inspection became totally divorced from advice, as the new OFSTED arrangements seemed to intend, schools would undoubtedly feel the loss of what they saw as an important aspect of inspection.

The changing role of LEAs

But this was too little and too late. A series of Conservative Secretaries of State in the early 1990s took the view that LEAs were not moving fast enough to implement a systematic process of inspection, or, if they were, the relationship between LEAs and their schools was too 'cosy' for the inspections to 'have teeth'. Following an influential political paper by the Conservative Chairman of LB Wandsworth's Education Committee (Lister 1991) and a professional paper by Wandsworth's Chief Inspector (Burchill 1991), the seeds of OFSTED were planted. OFSTED, not LEA inspectors, would be responsible for school inspecting nationally. LEAs were then in a difficult position, and their difficulties have increased since then. Many had hired and trained inspectors to perform the role which Kenneth Baker had outlined, but were then faced with an awkward choice: either they had to redeploy or get rid of their inspectors, or they had to 'lend' them to OFSTED for school inspections, leaving them vulnerable to charges of neglect of their LEA schools. Furthermore, legislation within the 1988 Education Reform Act promoted self-management of schools, and the handing-on by the LEA of increasing proportions of their overall education budget to the schools themselves. It looked, in 1993, as if LEAs were on the way out, and some LEAs began to plan for their own demise. A former LEA inspector herself, the new Secretary of State, Gillian Shephard, saw no obvious or immediate replacement for LEAs, and both Conservative and Labour Governments have since concentrated on making LEAs more aware of and responsive to the needs of their own schools, not least by introducing OFSTED inspections of LEAs. As the heads of individual schools ask for more and more of LEAs' budgets, so central government applies more and more pressure on LEAs' responsibilities to promote improvement in their schools' standards, both through inspection and through requirements reflected in the LEA / Schools Code of Practice (1999). LEAs generally are weakened, and caught in a sandwich between the two more powerful agencies, central government and the schools.

Many LEAs have, nevertheless, worked with their schools on a range of self-evaluation frameworks, and others have provided a range of training in evaluation for heads and other holders of responsibility in primary, secondary and special schools. Some have either undertaken or sponsored projects which are designed, amongst other things, to raise students' levels of achievement through the individual school's capacity to review its own performance, and take action on the basis of the quantitative or qualitative data collected. Good examples include projects undertaken by the London Boroughs of Hammersmith and Fulham (Myers 1996) and Lewisham (Stoll and Thomson 1996), Birmingham (Ribbins and Burridge 1994).

The NFER provides for schools and LEAs, through its Education Management Information Exchange (EMIE), an up-to-date summary of schemes of school self-evaluation to which LEAs have contributed, or which they have taken the lead in drawing up.

It is interesting to note that when Gray and Wilcox (1995) studied the extent to which LEAs involved school staff in the various aspects of the inspection process, there was considerable involvement (see Table 3.1). Gray and Wilcox conclude that the line between those carrying out inspections and those experiencing them was 'somewhat blurred' (p. 137).

One unusual development of the role of LEA inspectors was reflected in the Inner London Education Authority's (ILEA) 'Inspectors Based in Schools' (IBIS). ILEA inspectors based in primary or secondary schools modelled the process of self-evaluation and improvement. The stages in their work included:

- collection of information;
- sharing the agenda with schools;
- data-gathering and diagnosis;
- writing series of discussion documents, including examples of good practice;
- intensive period of inspector-led school-based INSET;
- evaluation and comment by school staff.

Table 3.1 Involvement by LEA of school staff in inspection activities

Aspect of inspection	Degree of involvement			
	None/minimal	*Some*	*Considerable*	*Not answered*
What to be inspected	28	41	27	4
How to be inspected	54	34	7	5
Collecting data	19	53	24	4
Analysing data	75	13	4	8
Content and recommendations of report	52	32	11	5

Source: Questionnaire to all English and Welsh LEAs ($n = 100$) 1992

For further details of the work of IBIS, see Jenkins (1987).

Now that LEAs themselves are subject to OFSTED inspections, OFSTED's purpose is to review and report on the way LEAs perform their functions and, in particular, to determine the contributions which LEA support, including support to individual pupils, makes to school improvements and to higher standards of achievement. I have already commented upon some of the potential hazards of OFSTED inspectors reporting on LEAs, and there is so far little evidence of OFSTED feeling the need to tread carefully in dangerous territory. The image chosen by David Singleton HMI (1998) to describe this activity is forthright: 'OFSTED is, we like to think, an opener of closet doors. What lies within may not always be pleasant, but we think the public has a right to see' (p. 8).

Finally, it is not clear whether, on the evidence of OFSTED's findings or not, central government envisages in the future a role for local government in schooling. LEAs are often presented in the media, and sometimes by head-teachers, as bureaucratic, slow-moving, insensitive and profligate with money which otherwise could go directly to the schools themselves. I find it both unfair and sad that central government and schools, having gained immensely more responsibilities and resources at the expense of LEAs, are now turning on the weaker partner in the alliance, and, often, finding fault in LEAs' performance when neither the resources nor the powers are available to LEAs to carry out their tasks effectively and efficiently. Speculating on the future role of local government, and perhaps on the emerging Regional Development Agencies, Peter Mortimore (2000) concludes:

> Loosening ties to a community enables a school to 'choose' its students on selfish grounds. Most schools will choose the 'easy to teach' rather than the 'hard to teach' students, who will end up clustered in the least attractive schools . . . the inevitable result will be that the current gap between the educational 'haves' and 'have nots' will increase still further . . . some local democratic control is important. Central government does not always know best what is good for schools and democratic communities must 'own' their schools in some way if they are to be genuinely democratic institutions rather than simply agents of national government. I am not opposed to varying the tier of local government – regions might play a key role in a devolved English system. I am opposed to the removal of some locally elected democratic influence.

TES 11 February 2000

Judged to be without a weakness

Inspectors failed to
find a fault in the
deprived borough of
Hammersmith and
Fulham, reports
Clare Dean

The context of school self-evaluation

John MacBeath (1999) has traced the development over the last few years of self-evaluation processes for schools, and many LEAs and individual educators are now producing useful manuals and frameworks for schools. For two useful recent versions, see National Association of Head Teachers (1999) and McCall (1998). Most headteachers have always sought to improve their schools, but systematic approaches became more frequent in the 1980s, often developed cooperatively by heads and LEAs. Two key documents were *Keeping the School Under Review* (1977), devised by Guy Rogers and other ILEA inspectors and *Guidelines for Review and Internal Development in Schools* (GRIDS) (McMahon *et al.* 1984). The provision for Local Management of Schools (LMS), a keystone of the 1988 Education Reform Act, further underlined a school's own responsibilities for monitoring and evaluating its own performance. Evaluation goes hand-in-hand with planning, and there has been a substantial increase in the amount and variety of ways in which schools undertake 'school development planning'. The purposes of development planning often include improvements in the quality of teaching and learning through the successful management of change.

Improvement in the quality of teaching and learning is at the heart of school improvement, and is particularly sensitive because it requires individual teachers to reflect on the strengths and weaknesses of their own performance and, probably, make changes: often this process entails classroom observation by colleagues or inspectors, and sometimes it makes use of students' own views on what helps them learn or what are the characteristics of good teaching. The whole process implies an openness and confidence in classroom teachers which currently many do not possess.

The development and use of 'indicators' of effectiveness by schools are not easy. One of the most intractable difficulties is that indicators are likely to be both quantitative and qualitative, and it is much easier to collect, analyse and interpret 'scores' – reading tests, end of Key Stage tests, GCSE results, attendance figures – than it is to evaluate the more general aims of many schools, such as developing their students as independent learners, or as knowledgeable and active participants in democratic life. Many schools are left struggling in the aftermath of the public disclosure of raw figures of academic or behavioural performance, which they consider unfair or incomplete. They would no doubt agree with the American maxim that we must learn to measure what we value rather than only valuing what we can easily measure.

Drawing on international comparisons, Louise Stoll and Dean Fink (1996) usefully summarise the most important considerations for schools (or other agencies) setting up indicators for self-evaluation:

- the purpose and audience for collecting information need to be clear;
- it is important to measure and acknowledge outcomes;
- performance indicators are only part of the whole-school story;
- there is a danger of overvaluing easily measured outcomes at the expense of ones less quantifiable;
- indicators should measure enduring features of schools so trends can be analysed over time;
- indicators should be understood by broad audiences;
- information should not be collected merely because it is available;
- indicators should address quality, equity and efficiency issues; and
- collecting too few indicators may lead to interpretation difficulties because of insufficient information. Too many can be overwhelming.

Above all, it is important that all those in the educational community see that information collected is used in some way to influence policy and practice. There are few things more frustrating for teachers than spending time contributing to huge banks of data which appear never to be used. Nor does testing itself, however regular and accurate, necessarily contribute to improvement: as the saying goes, you don't fatten the pig by weighing it.

School Evaluation Matters (OFSTED, 1998b) seeks to provide schools with a self-evaluation process parallel with the Framework. OFSTED is clear about its purpose, and how schools should organise their self-evaluation:

The booklet asks schools to answer four questions:

- how good is our school?
- what are our strengths and weaknesses?
- what must we do to improve?
- have we got what it takes?

Schools should have . . . a strategy for appraising their own performance which complements the thorough but occasional health check provided by inspection . . . independent inspection is here to stay. It is now an established and continuing part of school life . . . to be efficient, effective and complementary, evaluation by the school should draw from the criteria and indicators used in inspection, and should employ similar techniques. The inspection Framework sets out tried and tested rational criteria for the work of schools. This booklet shows schools how they can use the criteria to evaluate their own work.

OFSTED also gives each school a *Performance and Assessment* report (PANDA), which provides data as a basis for the school's self-evaluation. 'The Autumn Package' gives all schools the data needed for bench-marking purposes.

The role of 'critical friend'

In their analysis of the implications for schools and an LEA who were the subject of an OFSTED Accelerated Inspection Programme (AIP), Watling *et al.* (1998) outlined eight strategies for improving schools in difficulty, preferably instigated and supported by the LEA. These included both the provision of early, intensive outside support, and the 'withdrawal of external pressure/inspection in order to remove fear and give space to grow'. They believe that the LEA should act as 'crit-ical friend' and provide an appropriate balance between support and challenge.

The use of 'critical friends' to supplement school self-evaluation has also been developed, for example in Lewisham, London (Stoll and Thomson 1996). The role of the 'critical friend' has been well described as:

A trusted person who asks provocative questions, provides data to be examined through another lens, and offers critique of a person's work as a friend. A critical friend takes the time to fully under-stand the context of the work presented and the outcomes that the person or group is working toward. The friend is an advocate for the success of that work.

(Costa and Kallick 1993)

The use of 'critical friends' is one element in a broad partnership between LEA and school in supporting self-evaluation. The partner-ship has also been concerned to assess the effectiveness of the process by measuring gains in a variety of areas, including the development of teachers as learners, change in school culture and, significantly, in measures of student achievement. In one primary school, for example:

> The profile of academic achievement has already been raised. Standards of literacy continue the upward curve already begun before the Project started. The performance of Key Stage 1 children compared to National Curriculum norms is improving. Scores in the London Reading Test taken by Year 6 pupils show a decrease in the number of Band 3 children, with no change in pupil intake factors. The quality and range of writing, as judged by internal measures, has also been enhanced. The focus on analysing data on children's achievement is far greater and has pointed the school towards a more specific and sharpened focus on teaching and learning.
>
> (Stoll and Thomson 1996)

The role of the stakeholder

The previous sections have reviewed some aspects of the role played in school inspection and evaluation by the three agencies responsible for providing education: the national government (delegating its inspection function in England to an independent body in 1992), the LEA, and the school. This section explores the role played by other groups with a key interest in the process of inspection; teachers, governors, parents and school students themselves. Because schools are complex organisations involving continuous human interaction, and sometimes conflict, it may be that this section reflects more of the real experience of inspection than do the previous sections with their concern for formal purposes and procedures.

The OFSTED *Framework* does, of course, already provide access to the inspection process to all these groups. How effective such access is, how it is perceived by the groups themselves, how in reality it works, and how it might be developed are all important factors in relation to the primary purpose of inspection, school improvement.

Teachers

There are two key questions in this section. First, do the context and conduct of present national inspection arrangements mean that what inspectors learn from observing teachers' work and from their discussion with them provide an accurate and reliable picture of the quality of the contribution they make to school life? Second, do the oral and written reports present inspectors' judgements in such a way that teachers derive maximum benefit in improving the quality of their teaching and learning?

Although Chris Woodhead described OFSTED inspection simply as a 'health check', there is ample evidence to conclude that many teachers view an imminent inspection with anxiety, and in some cases terror. There is talk of 'them' coming to do something to 'us'. Anxieties have their roots in several perceptions:

- there may be a 'hidden agenda' to the inspection, and that inspectors are particularly keen to find negative aspects of teachers' performance;
- the inspection is an abnormal situation, the usual pattern of lessons will not be seen. What results is inevitably a superficial view of an artificial week;
- huge quantities of teachers' time and nervous energy are used in the preparation for inspection which might more constructively be used in school improvement;
- inspectors may be unsympathetic, inappropriately qualified, too busy (or all three) and that judgements will, therefore, not be fair;
- feedback after the observation of lessons and opportunities for professional discussion about matters of teaching and learning will be restricted or non-existent.

An important variable is how head-teachers prepare their colleagues for inspection: some seek to reassure their colleagues and keep the emotional temperature down, others use the situation to frighten them and demand changes in practice (Shaw *et al.* 1995). Although figures for head-teacher satisfaction with the part an OFSTED inspection plays in their school's development are high, the figures for classroom teachers are reported as lower. OFSTED (1994) has published conclusions for inspectors drawn from interviews with secondary school head-teachers

STILL HERE ?- THEY DIDN'T
TAKE UP MY SUGGESTION FROM
LAST TIME THEN .

and heads of department about what they think are the most helpful ways forward in school development.

HMCI's decision to add from the summer term of 1996 an 'adjunct' to the *Framework* whereby individual teachers are graded on the quality of their teaching has added another element of pressure on both teachers and inspectors. For some teachers, particularly those already anxious, the prospect of being individually graded becomes the largest, and most stressful, element in inspections. Inspectors are distracted from the complex and difficult task of assessing pupils' levels of attainment, what progress they are making, and the contribution which teaching is making to their progress, by having also to concentrate on teacher performance. The pressure on teachers to 'showcase' increases, and the prospect of the normal pattern of lessons being observed recedes even further. HMCI's justification of this extra pressure on individual teachers – 'reports to the Headteacher on particularly good or poor teaching will provide him/her with valuable management information from a source outside of the school' – seems particularly spurious. Identification of poor teachers is rarely a problem for a head-teacher: how to make them more effective, or how to get rid of them, are more relevant issues. In addition, normally 'good' teachers can produce poor lessons during an inspection, and incompetent teachers can often raise their performance for a short time. It's hard to escape the conclusion that HMCI simply wished to increase the pressure on classroom teachers. More directly, it makes it more difficult for school managers legitimately trying to develop a system for evaluating the quality of the school's work if classroom teachers associate such evaluation with the grading of individual teacher performance.

Under the present inspection circumstances, teachers are impeded from deriving full benefit from inspection by a variety of factors, which include:

- a context which is perceived by them as hostile, and in which they do not see themselves as 'partners';
- too few opportunities for professional discussion with inspectors on teaching and learning: what Wilcox (1992) defines as 'member checks' where the interpretations and conclusions of an evaluation can be tested with members of the groups from whom the data were collected; and
- the combination of a long-awaited, short and artificial basis for judgements, and what Ted Wragg and Tim Brighouse (1995) have called a 'lack of follow-up, continuity and aftercare'.

Teachers are key stakeholders in school improvement. If they are to make maximum use of the experience of inspection,

> teachers first have to be persuaded that the findings are 'true', then internalise them, and finally accept a share in collective responsibility for doing something about them.
>
> (Wilcox and Gray 1994)

Governors

It is not immediately clear whether an OFSTED inspection should be seen primarily as an inspection of a school including its governing body, or as an exercise being undertaken for the governing body. The brief answer is 'both'. Governors may influence the nature of an OFSTED inspection in a variety of ways:

- in exceptional circumstances, they may request a full inspection or a short one;
- before an inspection, they can bring to the attention of the registered inspector any particular issues of concern; and
- they can propose that particular features of the school, such as educational provision for the community, be included in the inspection.

Governors have various statutory duties related to the conduct of an inspection, such as arranging the meeting between parents and inspectors, and drawing up an action plan based on the inspection findings within forty working days, and making sure action is taken.

When judging how well a school is managed, inspectors must comment on how effectively the governing body fulfils its statutory duties in helping to shape the direction of the school, and whether it has a good understanding of the school's strengths and weaknesses.

Summing up their research on governing bodies and inspection, Creese and Earley (1999) conclude:

> The process of inspection is making it increasingly clear to governing bodies that they have an important responsibility to ensure that their school is effective and well-managed, and governing bodies – not only of 'failing schools' – are reconsidering how they currently perform their duties in the light of the inspector's report. The inspection process has empowered many governing bodies, particularly as they examine their role in relation to the post-OFSTED action plan. For some it has meant, perhaps for the first time, that they have had a meaningful involvement in the school and its decision-making and planning processes.
>
> (p. 87)

It may be worth drawing a distinction here between the generic process of inspection and the specific procedures of current OFSTED practice. While governing bodies generally welcome the concept of school inspection, their reaction to OFSTED is varied. The Institution for School and College Governors (ISCG 1996), for example, reports that inspection has been used in some schools as an improvement tool or yardstick, whereas in others it has been perceived as a 'weapon inflicting both pain and damage'. The ISCG report goes on to comment that under the intense scrutiny of an OFSTED inspection, governors may not have the language and confidence to articulate what they do. It then makes a critical point for the future relationship between governors and schools: it notes that a realistic approach is needed about what governors should be expected to do for no financial reward. The ISCG report also makes it clear that governing bodies should be aware of, and sympathetic to, what has been described as a post-OFSTED dip in performance. Research suggests that for weeks, months or even terms after an OFSTED inspection, there may be a dip in staff morale, energy and willingness to be involved in innovation or other change (Ferguson *et al.* 1999). Governing bodies may need to provide support to enable the school to regain its impetus, for example by providing targeted resources for staff development.

Finally, in their report on a much smaller sample of schools experiencing OFSTED, Lonsdale and Parsons (1998) comment:

> The general feeling from the governors interviewed in the study was support for the school and great scepticism about OFSTED:
>
> > '*In our action plan, in a polite way, we rejected their findings. So what – what are they going to do? – throw out all the governors?*' '*My view afterwards was "what was all the fuss about?" We don't need another of these.*'
>
> Others clearly felt that OFSTED was an inspection to find out what was wrong. Many accepted that there were some shortcomings within the school, but resented the idea the inspectors were coming in to tell them about these.

School students

OFSTED inspectors are currently required by 'The Framework' during an inspection to analyse samples of students' current and recent work, and to hold discussions with students about aspects of teaching and learning in the school. How high a priority 'the student voice' is within OFSTED's busy schedule varies from school to school, and OFSTED inspectors are normally sensitive to many other indicators of how seriously schools take the views of students about school and wider issues.

The potential power of 'the student voice' in school self-evaluation is well brought out by the Dutch school student quoted by John MacBeath (1999) who wished to contest an assertion by a head-teacher that 'she knew her school':

> I have sat in classrooms six periods a day for thirty weeks a year for five years and, with respect, I see things you could never see. These five years and thousands of hours are my life in school. They are my one chance.

(p. 16)

O.K. HE'S NO GREAT SHAKES, BUT WE LIKE HIM, SO WATCH IT!

Punch 1873

PENNY WISE.

National Schoolmaster (going round with Government Inspector). "WILKINS, HOW DO YOU BRING SHILLINGS INTO PENCE?"

Pupil. "'PLEASE, SIR, 'TAKES IT ROUND TO THE PUBLIC-'OUSE, SIR!!"

In reviewing their own provision, schools may in the past have been reluctant systematically to seek their students' views on which aspects of school life helped them learn, or did not. Perhaps some schools were unwilling to face up to the predicted answers; other felt that the task would be impossible without unprofessional comment about individual teachers.

Building particularly on the work of Jean Ruddock *et al.* (1996), many schools and research projects have developed procedures of building 'the student voice' into school self-evaluation. This process may well be further advanced by schools wishing to respond to the Government's requirement that elements of 'citizenship' be built into the curriculum and other aspects of school life. Opportunities for students to develop their views about teaching and learning, and other broader issues, and have them listened to by the school, are an obvious and desirable example of 'practical democracy' at work.

Amongst the most comprehensive and illuminating studies of 'the student voice' in school self-evaluation are the Improving School Effectiveness Project (ISEP) carried out in Scotland, and the Making Belfast Work: Raising School Standards (MBW: RSS project). The International School Effectiveness and Improvement Centre (ISEIC) in London was involved in both of these (see, respectively, Robertson and Sammons 1997 and Sammons *et al.* 1997).

Jon Pickering (1997) has summarised in a lucid and accessible way both the case for welcoming 'the student voice' into debates about school evaluation, and also some of the current obstacles which prevent this from happening fully.

Parents

Since the Local Management of Schools and the Parent's Charter, the power of parents in influencing the success of schools has been increased, and it is no surprise that from the beginning of OFSTED inspections, parents have been seen as key members of the school community whose views should be canvassed and further explored during inspection.

The main two sources of parents' views have been their responses to the OFSTED *Parents' Questionnaire* which governors are invited to send to all parents, and in the pre-inspection meeting with parents which is an

integral part of every inspection. A detailed analysis of parents'
responses to OFSTED inspection has been undertaken by Ouston and
Klenowski (1995) on behalf of Research and Information on State
Education (RISE), from whom an even fuller report is available (1995).

The analysis reflects what parents see as strengths and weaknesses in the process, as well as suggesting improvements and further areas for research or investigation.

Partly as a result of these comments by parents, and partly as a result of their own consultation procedures, OFSTED has sharpened the role of parents in the inspection procedure. From September 1997, registered inspectors must refer to any significant positive views or concerns expressed by parents and the inspection findings relating to them, both when reporting to the senior management team and the governing body, and in the inspection report. Schools may offer other evidence of parents' views about the school, and inspectors are required to evaluate it and use it. Inspectors are also encouraged to be accessible to meet groups or individual parents during an inspection, if they request a meeting. Emphasis is still placed on any evidence of the impact on standards achieved by partnership or contracts between schools and parents.

All stakeholders

Another way of analysing the views of separate groups of stakeholders is to compare each group with the others, and look for similarities and differences. Each group provides an important perspective for school self-evaluation, but taken together they may provide additional insights and prompts to action. An excellent example of this work is John MacBeath's project, commissioned by the National Union of Teachers, and reported on at two separate stages (MacBeath *et al.* 1996; MacBeath 1999).

MacBeath drew on the views of six groups of stakeholders – teachers, management, support staff, pupils, parents and governors – to compile a list of ten indicators which might form a framework for a school's self-evaluation. The indicators, well-supported by relevant research in the school effectiveness and improvement literature, are:

school climate	recognition of achievement
relationships	time and resources
classroom climate	organisation and communication
support for teaching	equity
support for learning	home-school links

It is interesting to note, as MacBeath does, that leadership and management were rarely mentioned as such in this study, though their effects may be implicit in many of the indicators suggested. Further exploration of these issues, and the use of stakeholders' perspectives in school self-evaluation, can be found in MacBeath (1999).

If a full picture of a school is to be assembled, it is clear that inspectors should seek the views of all stakeholders.

Conclusion

A surprising number of 'hot' issues in today's debates about school inspection have been in the public domain for many years. In reviewing past developments in the inspection process, I have outlined in this chapter arguments about the purposes of school inspection; the relative strengths and weaknesses of national and local inspectors in inspecting schools; the most appropriate relationship between inspector and teacher; the changing tensions within the inspector's role; the development of school self-evaluation, including the concept of 'the critical friend'; and the roles of the different stakeholders in the course of a school inspection. But though the questions have been asked before, the answers may well be different as we prepare a system of school inspection fit for the twenty-first century. Above all, what sort of inspection system will most effectively help schools improve? What's in it for schools?

QUESTIONS FOR FURTHER EXPLORATION

1　How well can a school inspector 'know' a school after one visit? Are regular visits by the same inspector desirable and feasible?

2　What part should 'local circumstances and difficulties' have in an inspector's report? How should inspectors report inadequacies which are not at all, or only partly, the responsibility of the school?

3　'Equals among equals': what should be the proper relationship between inspectors and teachers?

4   What are the main strengths and weaknesses of an LEA inspection of a school? Can an LEA inspector be both rigorous inspector and constructive adviser? How do these dual responsibilities compare with those of a head-teacher?

5   How could a school make the most use of an LEA inspector, or a team, based on the school site for a period of time?

6   What are the strengths and limitations of school self-evaluation?

7   Is the concept of a 'critical friend' useful in the evaluation of schools?

8   How should teachers, governors, school students and parents be involved in school self-evaluation?

9   Within a school, which aspects of self-evaluation should be carried out by peers and senior managers in a school? What role, if any, should the LEA and national inspectorate have?

10 What are the advantages of a national inspection system?

Daily Mail 5 September 1994

Schools watchdog attacks classroom failures who betray our children

SACK THE USELESS TEACHERS

BAD teachers must be purged if standards are to rise, the new education watchdog declares today.

EXCLUSIVE
By RAY MASSEY
Education Correspondent

4   Does inspection help schools in difficulty?

This chapter explores current inspection procedures for labelling schools in difficulty as 'failing', requiring 'special measures' or having 'serious weaknesses'. How helpful are these descriptions? What are the most effective ways of supporting such schools? How might their difficulties be anticipated at an earlier stage and prevented, or minimised?

The shock of greenery had surprised him. Spring's rain had forced the fresh foliage suddenly and its vivid greenness, seen from the motorway behind a hovering kestrel, had imprinted itself on his mind.

'What have we got then, Elliott?' barked Tallyforth, entering the boardroom of Æthelfleda High School in Tamworth, where the fingerprinters, the police photographer and the Mercian Police Force's forensic scientist Jake Clifford were busy at work.

Detective Sergeant Georgina Elliott, always and inevitably known as George, who was standing by the window overlooking the school's playing fields, looked up from her notebook. 'Hubert Stanton.' She indicated the body in the plastic bodybag stretched out on the floor. 'OFSTED Registered Inspector in charge of the inspection of Æthelfleda High School. Aged between fifty-five and sixty I would say. Found dead, slumped in that chair over there by the table at seven o'clock this morning.'

Tallyforth gazed blankly at the upright wooden chair and then around the sparsely-furnished room with its plain wallpapered walls, then turned towards Jake Clifford.

'Cause of death?' he demanded.

'Couldn't tell you that, Chief Inspector Tallyforth,' replied Clifford, a short

dapper man in a green lightweight suit. 'Too early to say. No obvious wounding. No gunshots. No abrasions. No sign of a struggle. Just possible it was natural causes. You know, heart attack or something. He was considerably overweight. But I'll have to examine his stomach back at the lab. and find his medical history before I can give you an answer. It could be poisoning. I've taken the contents of that coffee pot from over there.'

(From *Be a Falling Leaf* by Bob Bibby, Pierrepoint Press, 1998)

'Naming and shaming' of schools in difficulty

Inspection has always been seen as one way of raising standards in schools, and this has been a particular focus since the start of the new OFSTED arrangements in 1993. In identifying the strengths and weaknesses of schools, OFSTED inspectors from the start were likely to find schools where the levels of weakness were unacceptable – which required, in other words, 'special measures' to ensure their improvement. Another category of schools – those which are providing an acceptable standard of education but have 'serious weaknesses' – has recently been identified: in 1998 there were 3 per cent of schools in the first category, and about 10 per cent in the second (Woodhead 1998). 'Special measures' have been judged necessary in about the same proportion of primary and secondary schools (2 per cent), but in 7 per cent of special schools (OFSTED 2000d).

In 1998–9, a total of 193 schools were put into special measures either as a result of a Section 10 inspection or a follow-up inspection by HMI, whereas 230 improved sufficiently to be removed from special measures (OFSTED 2000d). OFSTED expressed concern at the number of schools failing what was for schools their second inspection and being put into special measures. What is particularly noticeable in the *Chief Inspector's Annual Report* is the assumption that schools can get out of special measures entirely through their own endeavours: there is no explicit acknowledgement of external factors, such as local or national policies, or socio-economic context. It's almost as if to mention these would be to encourage schools to use them as an 'excuse' for underachievement.

OFSTED is, however, clear about the first steps which schools need to take in getting out of special measures.

Once special measures are applied, handling the label of 'failure' is the first priority of the headteacher and staff. Teachers – and in some cases the pupils themselves – are left with negative feelings about their own worth. Governors also often react with shock, followed by anger. Restoring individuals' self-confidence, particularly among teachers and pupils, is crucial. Schools which recognise that they may experience emotions akin to grieving and take steps to cope with the feelings of bereavement have taken the first actions that will help to secure the school's rebirth. . . . Feelings of anger and resentment slow the process of recovery unless they are dissipated quickly. Morale can be damaged for a long time if the staff indulge in retrospective apportioning of blame.

(OFSTED 1999: 6)

The decision to create the category of schools 'requiring special measures' was apparently accompanied by an acknowledgement that, in the context of public inspection reports, it would be impossible, let alone undesirable, to keep these judgements secret or quiet: there has grown, unchecked, a context of 'naming and shaming', a policy which implies that public disclosure of 'failure' will be a spur to the school to improve quickly. As Caroline Lodge (1998) points out:

Public policy has used a rather blunt approach: improvement through continual scrutiny, public exposure and exhortation to emulate the most successful practice, assisted by a sharp dose of action planning and target setting, washed down with the threat of closure.

Schools judged to be 'requiring special measures' are not equally spread across the country. In their analysis of early OFSTED reports on secondary schools, Levacic and Glover (1994) concluded that schools in comparatively disadvantaged social contexts were more likely to have an adverse report with little attention paid to the institution's contextual problems or to those achievements which are less readily measurable in OFSTED's terms. Schools in areas of high socio-economic deprivation are more likely to be judged as 'failing'. OFSTED provides a socio-economic profile of each school's intake and local area: by this measure, schools drawing their intake from the least favoured socio-economic

Independent 11 June 1998

groups account for 17 per cent of schools throughout the country. Over two-thirds of schools judged to require special measures are in areas of striking social disadvantage, compared to the national 'failure' rate of 2–3 per cent. Secondary schools subject to special measures are predominantly, but not always, in areas of urban disadvantage. These figures make it clear that the validity of OFSTED inspectors' judgement about schools 'requiring special measures', and the belief that such a judgement is a spur to school improvement, both have to be set in the wider context of debates about definitions of 'failing' schools, or 'schools in difficulty'; about the quality of urban schooling; about the requirement to publish examination and test results; and about the over-all relationship of disadvantage to school students' patterns of achievement.

As I have suggested, the 'failure' of a school may be the end result of a complex interaction between school, LEA and national policies, and in the circumstances it is both unfair and counter-productive to put all the blame on an individual schools and its staff. The stories of Hackney Downs School in Hackney (O'Connor *et al.* 1999) and the Ridings School in Calderdale (Clark 1998) are excellent examples of the complexity of school failure.

'Troubled and troubling schools'

Commenting on the problems associated with the labelling of schools as 'failing', Kate Myers and Harvey Goldstein (1998) propose the term 'troubled and troubling' for schools that for a variety of reasons find themselves in difficulties. They go on to characterise three types of 'troubled' schools:

- *striving* schools are those that are in trouble but are determined to change and improve;
- *swaying* schools are ones where for a while it may be 'touch and go' whether the school will survive let alone improve in the face of their difficulties; and
- *sliding* schools are those that seem to have become fixed in a seem-ingly never-ending downward spiral.

Of course, these categories do not satisfactorily describe all schools in difficulty. Myers and Goldstein themselves point out that there are schools not doing as well as they might but not in a serious or even dire state, and that there are schools which are effective in some areas (e.g. departments in a secondary school) but not in others.

It may be helpful to group schools in these (or other) categories in order to determine the extent and nature of the support required, but, as Myers and Goldstein point out, each school is unique and will require its own individual blend of support in order for it to improve.

They also point out the inequity of putting the entire blame for 'fail-ure' on the school itself. Whatever is going on inside the school is often

Scotland on Sunday 29 July 1997

Hands up those who think schools get better when threatened with a big stick

John MacBeath, the only Scot on Blair's new Standards Task Force, begs to differ

compounded by circumstances which may be beyond the control of the school, for example, the level of support and resourcing, turnover of key personnel, local and national legislation, or the social deprivation of pupils and their families. OFSTED Frameworks have not allowed inspectors to take these external factors sufficiently into account.

Perhaps most interestingly of all, Myers and Goldstein consider 'failing schools' within the context of the use policy makers have made of school effectiveness research:

> Policy makers of most political persuasions choose to ignore the caveats and focus on the *prima facie* evidence of school differences as a means of avoiding responsibility themselves, and consequently laying the major responsibility for performance and hence for failure at the doors of the schools. Ironically, contextualising performance, by using adjusted tables of test scores, for example, may actually strengthen the belief that blame resides in the school by encouraging the view that *all* other factors have been accounted for, and that any residual variation *must* have its origins in the schools.
>
> (p. 184)

Finally, they point out that attributing blame does not necessarily help the situation get better. By lowering morale and thereby encouraging staff and pupils to leave, it may have the opposite effect.

'Failing schools, failing city'

These sober, academic voices are complemented by the more passionate, angry voices of classroom teachers in schools designated by OFSTED as requiring special measures. Martin Johnson (1999) argues that teachers in what he calls 'schools for the underclass' (defined as a school 'whose intake consistently contains a proportion of children of underclass origins sufficient to become the strongest single determinant of its life') have impossible tasks which are aggravated by the OFSTED system:

> OFSTED is an organisation established for political purposes. . . . It plays absolutely no part in improving school performance, because its role is to inspect rather than to advise. Its much-vaunted database is a fraud. It should be abolished in its present form, but of course it is too much of a political totem. . . . [The government] must end what amounts to victimisation of underclass schools. It must institute support for these schools and the communities they serve, rather than castigating them for failing to achieve impossible targets. My considered opinion is that working life in OFSTED failing schools is a living hell. . . I am angry at a society which first excludes millions of people, and then hounds those whose vocation is to support the excluded ones.
>
> (p. 117)

Implicit in these debates is the answer to another question often put by policy-makers; if some schools can succeed in difficult circumstances, why can't all? Schools do not have control over all factors which affect their performance, and, as Gewirtz *et al.* (1995) have shown, the impact of the quasi-market in school choice is making it harder for some schools to succeed, whatever their efforts, and increasing the gap between the rich and the poor in inner-city schools.

Observer 23 August 1998

School 'shame' squads fail exams test

by Martin Bright
Education Correspondent

Social mix

Thrupp (1999) argues that 'social mix' – the social class composition of a school's student intake – has a powerful impact on a school's process and on students' levels of achievement. He concludes from his research in New Zealand that the difference schools can make to student achievement is much less than often claimed by researchers working in school improvement or school effectiveness. School reform can therefore only play a small part in a situation which requires far broader social and political change.

> Many school processes which have been identified as contributing to student achievement may be less independent of school mix than researchers have typically allowed. Instead, aspects of schooling such as student relations, classroom instruction, and school organisation and management may be powerfully influenced by school mix. The likely effect of this will be to lift mean levels of student achievement in middle class settings and reduce mean levels of achievement in low socio-economic settings.
>
> (p.5)

Setting these ideas in the context of the 'politics of polarisation and blame', Thrupp goes on to make a key point in relation to the evaluation of schools in disadvantaged areas:

> By suggesting that schools are capable of being largely self-managing, self-evaluating and self-improving, . . . [school effectiveness and improvement] research may have underpinned decentralizing reforms which have removed important forms of administrative support and funding in the name of more autonomy for schools. The problem here is that although self-management may work for schools in middle class settings, researchers are likely to have underestimated the intense intake-related pressures which accrue to teachers and school leaders in working class settings and the effects of unequal resourcing, and so assumed that these schools can do more than they really can. Despite claims of the existence of exemplary low socio-economic schools, the school mix thesis suggests that decentralization could be expected to be much less successful in low socio-economic settings because of insufficient time, energy and material resources

to implement demands from central agencies or to undertake school improvements.

(p. 7)

Thrupp's important work draws on a sociological tradition which has explored the social factors which influence a student's, or school's, levels of achievement. He argues convincingly that some school effectiveness and improvement researchers have for too long ignored social factors, particularly social class, and analyses in detail the work of academics and others (including Michael Barber) from this perspective. His work draws on the earlier work of James Coleman (Coleman *et al.* 1966) in the United States, and in particular the relationship between achievement and what Coleman called 'social capital', the elements which a strong family contributes to a child's education.

> A child approaches the tasks set by the school with a set of attitudes mainly brought from the home. The child's performance, whether in handwriting, in multiplication tables, or in learning advanced algebra, depends not only on the opportunities and demands the school provides for doing well but also upon the desire, the goals, the attitudes, and the effect with which the child addresses these opportunities. The school has some effect on these latter qualities, but they are qualities that the child largely brings from home.

This does not mean, of course, that schools and other agencies are powerless to influence social capital. Jonathan Kozol (1991) has mapped out the territory of what he calls the 'savage inequalities' of children's lives, and Gene Maeroff (1998) has set out a constructive and exciting programme for increasing the social capital of children brought up in socially and economically deprived areas.

Educational disadvantage: how much can be expected of a school?

The relationship between disadvantage, standards in schools and school improvement is the subject of much research and fierce debate: for an excellent recent summary, see Mortimore and Whitty (1997). The central question in many of these debates is this: how much is it reasonable to expect a school to do in an area of social disadvantage? HMI inspection reports in the 1960s and 1970s suggested that there was often substantial underachievement in urban schools because insufficient academic demands were being made of students: there was a feeling that a 'caring school' was enough, and that the turbulence and social conditions in which many children lived meant that expectations of their learning had to be low. Important research, (e.g. Rutter *et al.* 1979) and Mortimore *et al.* (1988) showed that schools in urban areas *can* make a difference, and, given the same resources and distribution of pupil intake, one school in a disadvantaged area (or anywhere else, for that matter) can make more difference than another. These findings have led to a substantial body of research and inspection findings about the characteristics of these 'effective' schools (most accessibly summarised in Sammons *et al.* (1995). The further exploration of these effective characteristics is, in simple terms, the '*school effectiveness*' movement: *how* a school develops these characteristics – the management of change, including overcoming the obstacles – is essentially the business of the 'school improvement' movement.

There is now, quite rightly, a growing understanding that expectations of pupils in schools in disadvantaged areas should be as high as elsewhere. But what has accompanied the swing of the pendulum is the assumption that an urban school should succeed in fulfilling these expectations with resources broadly similar to other schools, rather than resources related to educational needs in that particular school.

OFSTED and social disadvantage

OFSTED appears ambivalent in the complexity of this debate. In one of its most impressive and important documents (OFSTED 1993) OFSTED comments on the limits of what individual schools can do:

> Most schools in these disadvantaged areas do not have within themselves the capacity for substantial renewal. The rising tide of national educational change is not lifting these boats. Beyond the school gate are underlying social issues such as poverty, unemployment, poor housing, inadequate health care and the frequent break-up of families. Education by itself can only do so much to

enable individuals to reach beyond the limiting contours of their personal social circumstances and succeed.

(p. 45)

It is the definition of 'so much' in that sentence which is at the heart of the debate. In a report on schools in the Manningham area of Bradford, OFSTED (1996) is also at pains to set the achievements of the schools in a social context, and to some extent – as far as it is politically able to do, perhaps – in the context of current educational national policies.

On the other hand, there is little flexibility within the normal OFSTED *Framework* to take account of the difficulties which schools in disadvantaged areas are likely to face (OFSTED 1995). Inspectors are certainly required to be aware of the social circumstances of the school they are inspecting, but the *Framework*'s criteria are consistent and national: there is little guidance for inspectors working in schools which have high proportions of children who, for a variety of reasons, are what Peter Mortimore calls 'hard to teach'. Nor does the OFSTED *Framework* allow inspectors to set these schools in the context of local and national policies by seeking and reporting the answers to very important questions: to what extent has an LEA offered support to the school, and how effectively has the school used such support? A school may be operating in an LEA which has had (or continues to have) a policy of selection, or a high proportion of grant-maintained schools, and may have been a secondary modern school linked in parents' minds with lower levels of academic achievement than local grammar schools. How should inspectors handle the difficult problem of local reputation? or the complex problem of parental choice? or the possibility that the school is trying to educate a sizeable number of students passed on (either through permanent exclusion or through more informal means) by more prestigious schools, perhaps anxious themselves for the maintenance of their public examination rates of success?

Reviewing research about the effectiveness of OFSTED reports in supporting school improvement in socially deprived areas, Law and Glover (1999) argue for the development of an inspection system which:

- pays greater attention to the particular context of each school as a learning community – using more than free school meals as the (only) key indicator of deprivation;

- allows greater credit to be given to marginal improvements as 'steps along the way' to enhanced outcomes;
- allows for more flexibility in reporting so that there is scope for greater celebration of success which can be used as a 'building block' within the local community;
- assesses the contribution made by the LEA and external agencies in securing changes in parental and community attitudes to school; and
- considers the secondary school as part of the progression from nursery to further education rather than as a self-contained unit in isolation.

The current presentation of OFSTED's judgement that a school requires special measures places all the responsibility on the school itself, and this is keenly felt by the teaching staff in the school. This is not to argue for a denial of responsibility (and this sometimes happens in schools which are in difficulty), but for the setting of an urban school's efforts in a wider context than the current *Framework* allows. Peter Mortimore and Geoff Whitty (1997) sum up the position succinctly:

> Demonstrating that opportunities for some disadvantaged pupils can be changed in particularly effective schools – even if the disadvantaged as a group remain behind their peers – can itself help to transform a culture of inertia or despair. It is this transformation that those who work in the field of school improvement are seeking. Schools with high proportions of disadvantaged pupils need extra support. Teachers who choose to work in these schools – because they want to help the disadvantaged – need their commitment recognised and supported rather than be 'blamed', as has happened so shamefully in the past.

> (p. 12)

'Commitment' on it own, of course, is not enough, and OFSTED is rightly concerned to improve the quality of teaching in all schools. But there is no doubt that it is more difficult to teach well in many urban schools than it is in other schools. My own experience of nearly twenty years in inspection convinces me that there are many teachers who are adjudged, quite accurately, to teach satisfactory or good lessons in 'other' schools who would not be able to achieve such grades in many urban

schools. Perhaps the OFSTED notion of 'quality of teaching' is too dis-
crete, and insufficiently related to the range of positive or negative
circumstances in which the teaching takes place: the extent to which, in
other words, a school enables good teaching to take place, or disables
teachers. It is also important not to see 'disadvantage' as too simple or
consistent a concept, or one for which the same response in schools is
always appropriate.

In OFSTED's review of '*Secondary Education, 1993–97*' (OFSTED
1998a) the performance of secondary schools in disadvantaged areas is
set out clearly, and analysed sympathetically, setting eligibility for free
school meals (FSM) against average GCSE points scores.

The key indicator for identifying social disadvantage in relation to schools is eligibility for free school meals. Although a single indicator, it correlates significantly with other indicators of social disadvantage recognised by the DfEE:

- 0.95 with eligibility for income support;
- 0.92 with children in large families with a lone parent;
- 0.91 with large families with no one employed;
- 0.74 with households where three or more children are in crowded accommodation, and
- 0.60 with children living in houses with no or shared WC/bath-room.

Over one and a half million children are eligible for free school meals, about one in five of the pupil population.

A GCSE points score can be calculated by allocating one point for a grade G, two for an F, up to eight for an A* for each subject taken at GCSE. Table 4.1, transposed from the graph in OFSTED (1998a) shows:

- there is an inverse link between the level of entitlement to free school meals and the proportion of pupils attaining higher grades at GCSE in comprehensive schools;
- improvement has taken place in all bands of free school meal enti-tlement, particularly those with 50–60 per cent and more than 60 per cent FSM eligibility; and
- the underlying differential between schools with 0–10 per cent FSM and schools with more than 60 per cent remains fundamentally the same.

In everyday terms, the table means that children in schools with 0–10 per cent FSM on average obtain better than six grade Bs and a D grade, while children in schools with more than 60 per cent FSM on average obtain the equivalent of four grade Cs and an F.

OFSTED point out another important aspect of the figures, not accessible from the table. For schools with the same level of disadvan-tage, average points scores differ widely. For example, schools with one fifth of the pupils eligible for free school meals (the national average) have average points scores ranging from twenty to forty-five points.

Table 4.1 GCSE average points score from 1993–6, grouped by free school meals (Comprehensive schools)

Free school meal eligibility (%)	*0–10*	*10–20*	*20–30*	*30–40*	*40–50*	*50–60*	*60+*
Number of schools	869	867	491	239	194	108	79
Average point score 1993	37.95	32.97	28.16	25.09	22.52	19.54	18.98
Average point score 1994	39.65	34.47	29.42	26.23	23.60	20.82	20.16
Average point score 1995	40.52	34.83	29.94	26.49	23.89	21.37	20.48
Average point score 1996	40.76	35.35	30.45	26.93	24.59	22.74	22.12
Points score difference: 1993–6	+2.81	+2.38	+2.29	+1.84	+2.07	+3.20	+3.14
improvement: 1993–6 (%)	7.40	7.22	8.13	7.33	9.19	16.38	16.54

Within the 3 per cent of schools with the highest percentage of FSM, the range of average points was eleven to thirty-six.

In their commentary on the figures, OFSTED point out:

> Schools in disadvantaged areas often receive pupils who have well below the national average attainment on entry . . . some of the schools serve populations that are very mobile and as a result lose and admit many pupils during the course of the year, increasing problems of educational discontinuity. Some of the pupils admitted may well have experienced difficulties in their school careers, in particular having been excluded from other schools. Other pupils may be newly arrived in Britain, with little or no English. Some of these pupils who are refugees may be traumatised, and others may lack any previous experience of school.

Commenting on the performance of schools which are subject to special measures, OFSTED goes on:

Attendance often falls below 85 per cent despite strenuous efforts by the school, raising levels usually proves time-consuming and the effort by the school is not matched by the pupils and their parents. Standards of behaviour are often satisfactory. However, in a small but insignificant number of schools, behaviour in classrooms and around the building is poor and pupils are vulnerable: here, inconsistencies in teachers' approach to behaviour management from lesson to lesson gives pupils too much scope for disruption. Levels of exclusion are, on average, three times the national average. Even where behaviour is good, pupils' attitudes and willingness to work are often poor.

There is in these quotations from OFSTED a clear acknowledgement that the time, efforts and skills of a school staff have to be seen, and taken into account, when making judgements in a wider local context. But until the publication of *Improving City Schools* (OFSTED 2000b) there seemed little appetite for exploring the implications for school inspection of the complex links between social disadvantage and educational achievement. Meanwhile, the National Commission on Education (1996) reported that there needed to be 'a concerted national policy' to tackle the raising of standards in disadvantaged areas, and that this policy might include a new approach to funding, attracting good teachers and encouraging local innovation.

Does OFSTED believe that its judgements that schools require special measures contribute to school improvement? The title of its recent publication, *From Failure to Success: How Special Measures are Helping Schools Improve* (OFSTED, 1997a) suggests that it does. Monitoring by HMI convinces OFSTED that the majority of schools under special measures are making satisfactory or good progress with addressing the key issues for action in their OFSTED inspection report. Indeed, OFSTED allows itself a pat on its own back (or a raspberry at the world of research):

Seven of these schools have improved and are now providing a satisfactory standard of education; they were subject to special measures for between two and three years, far less than the five-to-seven period which was cited by some researchers as the length of time required to turn a school round.

Four conditions for improvement are cited:

* accepting the judgement;
* knowing what to do;
* knowing how to go about it; and
* securing the support of all parties: the governors, teachers, pupils, parents and the LEA.

Michael Stark (1998) reflects the DfEE's agreement after working closely with OFSTED on 'failing' schools:

> It is our joint conclusion that the public identification of unacceptable standards tends to speed rather than delay recovery, and indeed is often a precondition for it.

Stark quotes the numbers of schools, judged by OFSTED to require special measures, which have been 'restored to health', or 'have made substantial progress', or are heading for closure. He also quotes OFSTED figures that it takes, on average, between twenty-four and thirty months for a secondary school to 'come out' of special measures – though he acknowledges this development as a 'return to competence' rather than 'the achievement of excellence'. He claims, too, that the recovery of failing schools after decades of weakness has brought new hope to other schools in like circumstances.

It seems vital, though, to separate the identification of unacceptable standards in a school from the automatic scapegoating of the school involved. Most people believe that all pupils have a right to the best possible education, and that inspection has an indispensable role in identifying educational provision which, for whatever reason, is unsatisfactory. However, the 'naming and shaming' of individual school communities is a crude, cruel and possibly counter-productive process in drawing inadequacies to the public's attention

Emotional reactions to 'special measures'

OFSTED's *Framework* and other documents often do not engage with those aspects of teachers' role which involve emotions. But it is clear that OFSTED inspections, and particularly verdicts of 'special measures', have a profound effect on some teachers' emotional lives. Peter Earley (1997), amongst others, likens the situation to a bereavement:

> People's reactions to traumatic events such as a death in the family are said to go through a number of stages. Inspection appears to be no different and the acronym SARAH usually describes the process experienced by most schools and governing bodies. It refers to the stages of: shock; anger; rejection; acceptance; help.
>
> (p. 390)

OFSTED recognises the depth of emotional disturbance which may take place, and is clear about what's to be done. ('Feelings of anger and resentment slow the process of recovery unless they are dissipated quickly . . . denial is often accompanied by blaming others' (OFSTED 1999: 6).

The use of the word 'denial' implies an alarming certainty about the correctness of a judgement requiring special measures. Such judgements may or may not reflect accurately the situation inside a school, but there are so many public questions about the validity and reliability of the OFSTED process that members of a school community may well reject a verdict of special measures. As Margaret Scanlon (1999) concludes from her research, it is often difficult for schools to accept special measures status when they have serious misgivings about the OFSTED system as a whole and/or the conduct of their own particular inspection. Scanlon's research pointed out that school students too may be emotion-

Metro 22 June 2000

School in crisis as teachers go

BY WENDY VUKOSA

ally affected: in some cases, students are abused by students from other schools who goad them with the taunt that they go to a useless school.

Finally, whatever the justification for the emotional distress which the OFSTED process may cause, there is something unsatisfactory about a procedure which may cause so much distress and then leaves someone else (LEA, consultant, families?) to rebuild and sustain the emotional resilience which it originally undermined. In response to inspectors' comments about 'the green shoots of recovery', one newly-appointed head responded:

> The effect of inspection initially was to almost stamp out those green shoots of recovery because of the damage which it did to us personally and I would argue that we would probably be in almost as good a position now if we hadn't had the inspection. What the inspection did, though, was actually to bring in a level of support from the LEA and, I guess, helped focus our minds in a way that we were able to implement change so speedily.
>
> (Scanlon 1999: 58)

School improvement and failing schools

Independent observers seem less confident than OFSTED about its contribution to improving schools. Describing a study of schools which had 'failed' their OFSTED inspection (Riley and Rowles 1997), Kathryn Riley (1998) notes:

> Contrary to assertions from OFSTED itself, there is no evidence that the OFSTED process itself improved schools . . . inspecting a school, or publishing information about it, is not the same as improving a school. For the future, we need a more defined and less costly rational audit of schools; local mechanisms for intervention; and a re-channelling of resources and energy into finding ways of identifying, challenging and supporting schools before they get into the downward spiral . . . undoubtedly, OFSTED has highlighted some major failures in the system, but it has rarely identified what was not already known.
>
> (p. 78)

She goes on properly to enquire why, if the state of the school was known, the LEA did not intervene more effectively. Did the LEA have the resources, human and financial, to support the school at an earlier stage?

Kathryn Riley also notes that 'school failure' is likely to result from a combination of national, local and school-based factors. Sometimes these factors are related. She found in the 'failing' schools studied a striking degree of teacher isolation: in one school in particular 'insular and fragmented and adrift from the usual range of professional inter-actions', and in another 'isolated from colleagues in other schools'. She notes that teachers themselves should take some responsibility for the sit-uation, but asks whether the previous Conservative Government policies which sought to establish schools as separate institutions which had to compete against each other for pupils ought not to share some of the responsibility. 'If schools themselves are seen as individual and separate units, it is not surprising that some teachers also behave in that way' (Riley 1998).

Riley's point about teacher isolation reflects an interesting, and influ-ential, distinction pointed out by Susan Rosenholtz (1989). In her study of *Teachers' Workplace*, she differentiated between schools where there was high-consensus within the teaching staff, and those low-consensus schools where few teachers seemed attached to anything or anybody, and were more concerned with their own identity than a sense of shared community. Teachers in such schools often displaced their sense of frus-tration by blaming their students, while they themselves remained apart and aloof. Rosenholtz refers to such schools as 'stuck' (as opposed to healthy 'moving' schools): teachers created environments in which they felt trapped – 'boredom, punitiveness and self-defensiveness resulted'.

In developing this view of 'stuck' schools as a separate category, David Reynolds (1995) suggests that 'failure' may have its own characteristics rather than being simply an absence of success. Drawing on his own work with such schools, he concludes that they have a number of 'patho-logical characteristics':

- they do not possess the basic competencies to do what it is they need to do to improve;
- their teachers may project their own inadequacies on to the chil-dren which enables the school to retain a perception of itself as normal and to blame the children for its failings;

Observer 9 September 1996

Teachers go sick as inspectors pile on pressure

Martin Bright

- they possess numerous fantasies, that change is someone else's job and that the school should carry on as it has been because things have always been done that way;
- they fear failure and staff are reluctant to take the risks that successful change involves, fearing that failed attempts to change will damage them;
- they do not know enough about alternative policies, how the school functions, the ways to change and the ways to relate to sources of outside help;
- they fear the school's failure being exposed to public gaze, a fear which will be often behind a 'macho' façade of apparent security;
- they have grossly dysfunctional sets of interpersonal relationships. Numerous personality clashes, feuds, personal agendas and cliques make rational decision-making very difficult. The tendency will be for staff to take stands on issues, even on vitally important ones, based upon reactive views of the personalities and groups putting forward proposals rather than on the intrinsic merits of the proposal.

So how can schools with these 'pathological characteristics' be helped to improve? Reynolds's advice is that:

We may need to direct them, to rid ourselves of the dangerous nonsense that they will somehow discover what's needed to succeed if we cane them through market pressures and public vilification. The building of any effective school requires foundations, which in the case of these schools means staff learning planning, management and pedagogic skills.

Reynolds believes that debating the goals of change, or longer-term planning, is not immediately helpful to such schools: the most important thing in the ineffective school may be for the staff to do something, and think later about the broader picture. In the longer-term, he concludes, these schools need more complex, more psychologically aware and above all more informed interventions than those that are currently on offer.

In a later piece, Reynolds (1998) makes some positive suggestions about what these 'interventions' might be. In summary:

- ineffective schools need information on how to improve themselves, imported perhaps by an individual member of staff, or group, familiar with research and practice in school improvement;
- rebuilding interpersonal relationships within the staff;
- the need to marshal as many 'reinforcers' of change as possible, including evidence from parents and pupils;
- the development and use of micro-political skills to manage power effectively and build necessary coalitions;
- goals should be chosen that are both easily achievable, and achievable in a short time;
- schools should be given the truth about their situation, otherwise known as 'brute sanity' (Fullan 1991); this might be brought, for example, by external consultants.

Reynolds also has some interesting, and provocative, suggestions about the direction teacher development should take if ineffective schools are to be 'turned around'. Noting that British methods of teacher development have traditionally been concerned with a 'voluntaristic approach' in which the technologies of education are chosen by individual teachers and head-teachers from a range of strategies, he suggests:

Whilst the generation of their own individual methods may be responsible for the 'artistry' of the leading edge of British teachers and schools that has historically been much commented upon, it is possible that it may also be responsible for the 'trailing edge' of British practice also seen in the ineffective schools. Methods utilised in other societies whereby good practices in teaching and in schooling are discovered, codified and routinely transmitted as part of the routine procedures of professional education, may have positive effects, therefore, on our educational variation in general and upon our ineffective schools in particular.

The priority for action rather than debate or planning was also emphasised by Karen Seashore Louis and Matt Miles (1992) in their work on improving American urban high schools:

In 'depressed schools' one of the few ways of building commitment to a reform programme is for successful action to occur that actualises hope for genuine change. Effective action by a small group often stimulates an interest in planning rather than vice versa.

In a very positive report on schools in urban areas which appear to cope better than others with different external circumstances, OFSTED (2000b) set out the general characteristics of these more effective schools:

No peculiar set of ingredients for improvement emerges from the survey. The same ingredients are potent in the mix in these schools as in any others: strong management, a well organised and focused curriculum; good teaching; close monitoring and effective personal support of pupils; and good links with parents – all based on high expectations of what it is possible for pupils to achieve. What is distinctive is the single-mindedness of the approach: the clarity; intensity and persistence of the schools' work, and the rigour with which it is scrutinised. At the centre of that work lie a determination to give close attention to individual needs and progress, and a commitment to ensuring that all pupils, including those from minority ethnic groups and others at risk of under-achievement, participate in and benefit from school activities. In these respects, across all key areas, the schools do well what can be done more easily in less exacting conditions elsewhere. They master the art of connecting work on different parts of the school's provision, so that action, informed by a clear and common purpose, is concerted and coherent. The result is greater consistency between policy and reality, and in the practice of staff, than is common elsewhere.

(p. 15)

But the writers of the report do not make the mistake of assuming that the efforts of the school community are enough:

What is clear from inspections is, first, that the variations in funding from school to school are to a considerable degree unfair, and, second, that some schools do not have enough money to do a good job.

(p. 40)

Schools in special measures and the LEA

OFSTED is also clear about the kind of support which helps schools in special measures:

Typically, there is a link adviser who has an important role in providing or organising appropriate training for staff, including the managers. In schools where there is an initial high level of consistent, well-directed support from the same advisers, progress is forthcoming. LEAs need to prioritise what needs to be done and then concentrate on those priorities. They also need to take swift action when the leadership of the school is weak. OFSTED caution against 'excessive monitoring', for example of the quality of teaching, without providing any help that results in better practice in the classroom.

(OFSTED 2000d)

Donald Fisher (1999) has drawn together a comprehensive and accessible compilation of ways in which, in partnership with schools, LEAs can provide support for underachieving schools.

QUESTIONS FOR FURTHER EXPLORATION

1   What are the advantages and disadvantages of labelling schools as 'failing', 'requiring special measures', or having 'serious weaknesses'? Are the interests of the individual school, the education system and society at large equally served by the categorisations?

2   In a national inspection system, what allowances, if any, should be made for schools which serve areas of social disadvantage, or which have high proportions of students who are 'difficult to teach'? How should inspectors take into account the social mix of a school?'

3   Which aspects of current OFSTED methodology are sufficiently valid and reliable that a verdict of special measures can be trusted?

4   Is the 'failing school' the most appropriate description if improvement is to take place? In secondary schools, the work of Pam Sammons and her colleagues (Sammons *et al.* 1998) suggests wide variations in departmental performance. Should departments which are well-managed and where students are achieving well be included in the designation of a 'failing school'?

5   Heads and teachers report shock and traumatisation of their school community when a verdict of 'special measures' is given. Is this experience a necessary purge ('You have to break a few eggs to make an omelette', as one OFSTED inspector put it) before cleansing and recuperation can take place? Or does it hinder the process of improvement by further demoralising communities already in difficulty?

6   At what stage in a school's development is external inspection likely to be most effective in promoting improvement? What's in it for schools in external inspection?

7   What other forms of inspection or audit would be more effective (and more efficient in time, energy and resources) in identifying and supporting schools in difficulty?

8   What effects are verdicts of 'special measures' or 'serious weaknesses' likely to have on school improvement?

5 Does inspection help schools improve?

In this chapter inspection arrangements are set in the context of what we know, both from school improvement research and from practical experience, helps schools improve their performance. Where does inspection fit in?

One day, after I had spent some months in the infants' department, a lady inspector appeared in class with the headmistress. Miss Wilkie, our teacher, told us to sit up straight, fold arms and listen. At other times, to ensure complete silence in class, this lady clicked a small wooden instrument called a 'signal', upon which we all placed a forefinger across our lips, pointing up a nostril, and stayed that way until she signalled release. The visitor addressed the fifty of us very sweetly and ended by asking me to stand on the form and read aloud from a primer. This I did, after which the headmistress presented me with a book, the 'progress prize', she said, 'for the little boy who has learnt to read the quickest in the whole class'! The inspector smiled and smiled.

I rushed home. Mother was with a neighbour, but I babbled it all to my sisters. Their reaction staggered me. Even Ellie, the essence of good nature, seemed displeased. And Janie was scathing. 'You could read very well before you ever went near the Infants!' This was true; all we younger children had been pupils in a perpetual seminary which the girls ran in various corners of the kitchen. Even by the time I was three Ellie had cut letters out of shop showcards and got me building words with her mobile alphabet. In a huddle the girls now discussed the affair, while I stood apart, apprehensive. Then Janie came up. 'You're a cheat! That's what you are! That book's going back! Give it to me!' I pushed it

> *tightly under my armpit, broke into tears, called them names and settled myself*
> *miserably on the stair bottom.*

> From *A Ragged Schooling* by Robert Roberts,
> Fontana, 1979

School and social context

In reviewing his work for over twenty years in school improvement, Peter Mortimore (1998) presents his position as asserting 'the potency of the individual school whilst also recognising the limitations of its social context'. Exploring the characteristics of the 'potent' school, and the processes through which it becomes more potent in influencing its students' educational outcomes, has essentially been the business of the school effectiveness and school improvement movements over the last thirty years.

The precise balance between 'the potency of the individual school' and 'the limitations of its social context' is both complex and elusive. Researchers who broadly subscribe to school effectiveness or school improvement approaches tend to concentrate on the former, sociologists on the latter. Many sociologists of education believe that school effectiveness research is particularly vulnerable to political take-over, partly because (they say) such research suggests that financial resources don't matter, and partly because the fact that some schools with similar intakes appear to be 'doing better' than others can be used by politicians to castigate less effective schools. Teachers, too, may feel ambivalent about such research:

> For teachers effective school research has been a two-edged sword. It has raised the possibility that they can make a difference to educational outcomes [but] . . . in the post-Reagan and Thatcher eras it has also saddled them with responsibilities over which they would claim to have little control. . . . At the height of the implementation of the New Right agenda, the claim that schools could make a difference was used ideologically to deny any suggestions that schools were limited in their performance by their socio-economic intake or context.

> (Lauder *et al.* 1998)

From the classroom teacher's point of view, Martin Johnson (1999) reminds us of the boundaries of what individual teachers and schools can do:

> The whole focus within school improvement is on what teachers do. It is argued that improvement in results occurs when the teachers work harder, change their practices, raise their expectations of pupils, and so on. In the real world, however, the usual way to improve results is actually to import some pupils from more favoured backgrounds; the trick is how to achieve that. The truth is that the same teacher using the same methods achieves vastly different results in two different schools. We all know this, and it does not help when the whole of current educational policy seems to depend on its denial.
>
> (p. 9)

School effectiveness and school improvement

This work did not start, however, with a focus on 'educational outcomes'. As a young teacher in London, I grew up within the sociological tradition which suggested that class and parental attitudes to education were the most important variables in determining young people's success in their schooling (e.g. Douglas 1964). The discipline of educational sociology gave this generation of teachers great insight into the ways the social context of communities influenced pupils' progress in both academic subjects and in behavioural or attitudinal development. But in so doing it undermined, sometimes explicitly, sometimes implicitly, the capacity of the school to make a difference to how much pupils might achieve. This was particularly true of pupils from socially disadvantaged areas: teachers often accepted a crude and distilled version of the findings of educational sociology, which they interpreted as showing that the more disadvantaged a community, the less could be expected of its pupils academically.

I remember the excitement with which I read in the magazine *New Society* of the work of Michael Power and his colleagues on juvenile delinquency (1967), which provided clear evidence from a study involving twenty secondary modern schools in Tower Hamlets that some schools were able to protect their boys from delinquency while others seemed to put their pupils at risk. Schools <u>could</u> make a difference! David Reynolds (1976) built on this work in his study of delinquency and schools in a disadvantaged South Wales community. The focus of this tradition was broadened in the study published by Michael Rutter *et al.* (1979), *Fifteen Thousand Hours*, which concluded that:

> schools do indeed have an important impact on children's development, and it does matter which school a child attends. Moreover, the results provide strong indications of what are the particular features of school organisation and functioning which make for success.

The 'particular features of school organisation and functioning which make for success' have been the subject of school effectiveness research ever since, and the processes through which these features may be developed have been studied by school improvement researchers.

'School effectiveness' and 'school improvement' are not necessarily complementary, however. Reynolds and Stoll (1996) note that the two traditions are quite distinctive, and that 'school improvers' often do not seem to base their strategies on what has been learnt from school effectiveness research.

In their recent review of research about school improvement, Gray *et al.* (1999) helpfully set out the differences between school effectiveness and school inspection. These are set out in Figures 5.1 and 5.2.

It would be wrong to conclude that schools have moved forward hand-in-hand with school improvement research. Many who work in schools, or are in regular contact with schools, have found relevant research inaccessible or of poor quality, or both. Researchers are portrayed as 'out-of-touch' with the pressures and unpredictabilities of daily life in a classroom, or unsympathetic to the detailed definition of the characteristics of effective teaching and learning. Researchers such as Michael Fullan and Andy Hargreaves in Canada, and Laurence Stenhouse and John Elliott in the UK, have argued that school improvement will not be consistently effective until teachers are more involved in the process of research, and become 'teacher-researchers' themselves. Lack of time is obviously the biggest obstacle to this development, but there have been encouraging signs that some teachers are putting into practice the procedures inherent in Donald Schon's concept of the

---

- A bottom-up orientation – school improvement should be 'owned' by the individual school and its staff
- A concern with organisational and cultural *processes* rather than in the *outcomes* of the school – it is the 'journey' which matters
- A perspective which views educational outcomes as inherently problematic, requiring the discussion and adoption of goals at school level
- A more qualitative orientation in its research methodology – the main data needed for improvement should reflect the views of the key participants
- An interest in seeing schools as dynamic institutions requiring extended study over time rather than the typical 'snapshots' which have characterised most cross-sectional studies
- A focus upon 'school culture' rather than the 'school structure' as the main way of understanding the potential for school growth and development

---

Figure 5.1 The school improvement tradition

- Focus on outcomes
- Formal organisation and structure, rather than culture
- Characteristics of already effective schools
- Schools as static organisations
- Commitment to quantitative methods
- School effects over time
- Consistency of school effects in different outcomes
- Differential effectiveness for different groups of students
- Primary/secondary school sector influence on pupils' progress over time
- Multi-level modelling (10–15 per cent variation in pupils' achievement may be accounted for by educational influences)
- Departmental differences

Figure 5.2 The school effectiveness tradition

'reflective practitioner', which has been further developed by researchers such as David Frost in 'reflective action planning'. This change in the teacher's role to include the capacity to undertake research implies further training, and several accredited courses at Diploma and Master's level now include opportunities for teachers both to learn about research procedures and to undertake action research in their own schools. The Teacher Training Agency (TTA) has provided welcome support for these developments through its Teacher as Researcher scheme.

In reviewing the contribution of educational research to the cause of school improvement, John Gray (1998) concludes:

- a good deal more of the variation in pupils' performance lies *within* schools than *between* them; most schools have pupils who are doing well with respect to national norms as well as pupils who are doing badly;
- schools usually account for between 10–15 per cent of the variation in pupils' performances; and
- around 1 in 18 schools may be doing well, given their intakes, whilst a similar proportion may be doing badly; the greater bulk of schools (between two-thirds and three-quarters) are, however, performing around the levels one would predict from knowledge of their pupils' starting points;
- there is great variability in the performance of subject departments within [secondary] schools; only a minority of schools do well across the board; the greater majority have stronger and weaker departments.

(pp. 5–6)

Gray's conclusions, which are supported by Pam Sammons *et al.*'s recent research (1997), are of crucial importance in thinking about the future of school evaluation. If the greater variation in pupils' performance lies within schools rather than between them, then the whole-school OFSTED inspection is revealed as unfocused, inflexible and expensive. Individual schools, and their LEAs, have an important responsibility to be aware of these variations, and to share learning from the particularly effective as well as to take remedial action in the case of the ineffective.

Approaches to school improvement

How do schools approach school improvement? The impetus may come from within the school, from the arrival of a new head-teacher, or from pressure from outside such as an inspection. School improvement has been defined as:

> a systematic, sustained effort aimed at change in learning conditions and other related internal conditions in one or more schools, with the ultimate aim of accomplishing educational goals more effectively.
>
> (Miles and Ekholm 1985)

This definition gives priority to 'aims' and to the processes of change. In today's circumstances, with the general emphasis on 'outcomes', it should perhaps be set alongside a more pragmatic definition drawn from the Improving Schools Project (Gray *et al.* 1999).

> An 'improving' school in our study was one which increased in its effectiveness over time. In other words, the amounts of 'value-added' it generated for its pupils would be expected to rise for successive cohorts.
>
> (p. 5)

In their seminal book on school improvement, Stoll and Fink (1996) define it as a series of concurrent and recurrent processes in which a school:

- enhances pupil outcomes;
- focuses on teaching and learning;
- builds the capacity to take charge of change regardless of its source;
- defines its own direction;
- assesses its current culture and works to develop positive cultural norms;
- has strategies to achieve its goals;
- addresses the internal conditions that enhance change;
- maintains momentum during periods of turbulence;

- monitors and evaluates its process, progress, achievement and development.

(p. 43)

Bruce Joyce (1991) used the term 'doors' to describe different ways in which a school might get started on school improvement. Louise Stoll and Peter Mortimore (1995) developed the list to include both *internal* and *external* doors.

Internal doors include:

- *collegiality* – the development of cohesive and professional relations within and beyond schools, and efforts to improve the culture of the schools;
- *research* – the use of research findings on school and classroom effectiveness and school improvement;
- *self-evaluation* – the collection and analysis of school and student data, action research in classrooms and staff appraisal;
- *curriculum* – the introduction of self-chosen curricular or cross-curricular changes or projects;
- *teaching and learning* – the study, discussion and development of teaching skills and strategies (such as flexible learning and cooperative group work);
- *partnerships* – activities and projects that involve parents, community representatives and agencies, LEAs, business and industry, higher education, Training and Enterprise Councils, and educational consultants;
- *school development planning.*

External doors include:

- *inspection*;
- *provision of 'value-added' data* by LEAs, OFSTED or other agencies;
- *projects initiated by external agencies*;
- *'quality' approaches*, often based originally in business or industry, such as *Total Quality Management* (TQM) and *Investors in People* (IIP);
- *National Curriculum and assessment developments*;
- *other national initiatives*, such as teacher appraisal, or the *National Literacy Strategy*.

There is continuing debate as to whether improvements pressed, or even mandated, from outside are as effective in the long term as those initiated internally.

Roland Barth (1990) describes two different approaches to school improvement, the first of which appears uncannily like the current Government and OFSTED approach. Assumptions in this approach are:

- schools do not have the capacity or the will to improve themselves; improvements must therefore come from sources outside the school;
- what needs to be improved about schools is the level of pupil performance and achievement, best measured by standardised tasks;
- schools can be found in which pupils are achieving beyond what might be predicted. By observing these schools, we can characterise their characteristics as 'desirable';
- teachers and heads in other schools can be trained to display the desirable traits of their counterparts in high-achieving schools. Then their pupils too will excel;
- school improvement, then, is an attempt to identify what school people should know and be able to do, and to devise ways to get them to know and do it.

(p. 38)

Barth's preferred approach is very different, basically relying on the skills, aspirations and energy of those who work in schools. The assumptions in this approach are:

- schools have the capacity to improve themselves, if the conditions are right. A major responsibility of those outside the school is to help provide these conditions for those inside;
- when the need and purpose are there, when the conditions are there, adults and students alike learn and each energises and contributes to the learning of the other;
- what needs to be improved about schools is their culture, the quality of interpersonal relationships, and the nature and quality of learning experience;

- school improvement is an effort to determine and provide, from without and within, conditions under which the adults and youngsters who inhabit schools will promote and sustain learning among themselves.

(p. 45)

The right balance of internal and external impetus may vary from school to school, or in the same school from time to time. Teddlie and Stringfield (1993) argue that a basic level of school effectiveness is necessary before the implementation of a school improvement programme, whether internally or externally devised. Schools which have not achieved this level may require sustained and targeted support early in the programme. Reynolds (1976) makes a similar point: the problems of a school in real difficulties may not be resolved by seeking to develop the characteristics of an effective school. There may need to be some more basic therapy first.

Key factors in school improvement

Four key factors emerge from the research on school effectiveness and improvement:

- quality of leadership;
- managing change in the 'culture' of the school;
- focus on teaching and learning;
- systematic professional development of staff.

Quality of leadership

Different theories of school leadership crop up in most school improvement work. Stoll and Fink (1996) provide an accessible summary before contributing their own phrase – 'invitational leadership'.

Leadership is about communicating invitational messages to individuals and groups with whom leaders interact in order to build and act on a shared and evolving vision of enhanced educational experiences for pupils.

(p. 109)

There are several attractive features of this definition. First, 'invitations' are messages communicated to people which inform them that they are able, responsible and worthwhile: they are to do with optimism, respect and trust. Second, the definition differentiates both individuals and groups. Third, it makes clear that creating a vision – even one that is shared, not personally devised – is not enough: it has to be acted upon. Finally, leadership activities and styles are seen only as a means to an end – the end being a better education for pupils.

The recent establishment of national training for existing head-teachers and for those aspiring to be heads (*National Professional Qualification for Headship*) by the TTA has meant that heads themselves have increasingly been consulted and involved in processes designed to improve the quality of leadership in schools.

Selecting the heads of sixty-seven schools where leadership had been commended by OFSTED, Lawlor and Sills (1999) asked them to identify those characteristics of head-teachers which are most significant in successfully effecting school outcomes. In compiling the list of characteristics, they drew on the 'competence' tradition, founded by McClelland (1987) and developed by others, including HayMcBer. The characteristics most frequently chosen were:

- the ability to work simultaneously on a variety of issues and problems;
- has clear, shared values and vision;
- passion for pupils' development and achievement;
- understands the need for, and practises, well developed inter-personal skills;
- sets high expectations;
- uses monitoring and evaluation for improvement;
- prepared to take risks;
- high levels of knowledge, understanding and professional confidence;
- appropriate use of structures and systems;
- efficient use of time;
- political awareness and skills;
- integrated approach to strategic and operational issues;
- whole school perspective and approach;

- positive commitment to staff development;

(pp. 54–5)

These responses emphasise the importance of context in influencing leadership style and the balance of qualities which a school leader may require in order to operate effectively. There appears to be little support for the 'strong, charismatic personality' model of school leader.

Stark (1998) agrees that charisma on its own is neither necessary nor sufficient. Looking at OFSTED/DfEE evidence on the qualities of head-teachers who have 'led their schools to improvement', he sets out a key set of skills:

- *strategic skills*: formulating (or helping governors to formulate) an overall vision for the future of the school: and within it, identifying strategic targets and prioritising between them;
- *monitoring skills*: keeping tabs on the crucial points where improvement is needed, including classroom observation of colleagues' teaching as a constructive rather than oppressive technique;
- *collegiate skills*: enabling the governors to work as a cohesive, focused unit; creating a sense of common purpose and identity amongst teaching colleagues. This includes the crucial trait of being 'approachable';
- *staff management skills*: including gaining the co-operation and respect of colleagues, and if necessary taking and implementing tough decisions about early retirement and competency proceedings;
- *staff development skills*: planning the personal development of other teachers to give them the skills they need to raise standards;
- *resource management skills*: relating limited means (financial and staffing) to strategic ends, and matching the priorities, and ensuring proper resource control; and
- *ambassadorial skills*: representing the school's interests to the LEA, diocese or other body, and negotiating their support; and more widely, presenting its public face to parents and the local community (particularly to local newspapers) to regenerate public confidence.

(p. 40)

The sensitive interplay between leader and social context, or 'culture', is integral to the definition of 'educative leadership' proposed by Duignan and Macpherson (1992):

> educative leadership is part of the process of modifying or maintaining an organisational culture. . . . Educative leadership helps to articulate, define and strengthen those enduring values, beliefs and cultural characteristics that give an organisation its unique identity in the minds of participants . . . educative leaders use the tools of culture to build an ethos, to create shared assumptions about responsibilities and relationships, and to gain the commitment of groups to the achievement of tangible and intangible goals and objectives.

An important point within this definition is the recognition of the individual school's 'unique identity', and of the leader's responsibility to be sensitive to its culture.

Managing change in the culture of the school

Within the management of change in any school, some processes are easier to define (though not necessarily to implement) than others. 'Organisational change' and 'development planning' are two examples which are relatively unambiguous and are commonly understood within school communities. While the 'culture' of a school is more complex, it may be equally important to understand and be able to change it if the school is to make progress. Definitions vary from the simple and practical – 'the way we do things here' (Deal and Kennedy 1983) – to the complex and theoretical (e.g. Schein 1985). In summing up his view, Schein argues:

> that the term 'culture' should be reserved for the deeper level of basic assumptions and beliefs that are shared by members of an organisation, that operate unconsciously, and that define in a basic 'taken-for-granted' fashion an organisation's view of itself and its environment.

(p. 6)

There have been various attempts to categorise different types of school culture. Amongst the best-known are Rosenholtz's (1989) 'moving' and 'stuck' schools; the development of this distinction by Hopkins *et al.* (1994) into 'moving', 'stuck', 'wandering', and 'promenading' schools; and Stoll and Fink's (1996) further development into 'moving', 'cruising', strolling', 'struggling', and 'sinking' schools.

While these distinctions are helpful, many schools appear to have elements in them which fit more than one category. Or they have conflicting sub-cultures (e.g. subject departments in a secondary school); sometimes schools are seeking to impose one culture (e.g. a commitment to academic achievement) against the resistance of another (e.g. a predominant pupil culture emphasising that it is not 'cool' to achieve according to traditional academic criteria). In most schools, it takes time and skill to identify accurately the cultural map, and to take its variations into account while planning progress.

Drawing on research literature and their own professional experience, Stoll and Fink (1996) set out the cultural norms which underpin successful school improvement:

- *shared goals*;
- *responsibility for success*;
- *collegiality*;
- *a belief in continuous improvement*;
- *lifelong learning for children and adults*;
- *risk-taking as an essential part of growth*;
- *mutual support*;
- *mutual respect*;
- *openness*;
- *celebration and humour*.

(pp. 92–7)

Because cultures depend on beliefs, assumptions and values, they are likely to be less accessible than behaviour patterns (or responses to uniform questions) to those seeking to make schools more effective. Yet it is clear from theory, research and practical experience that the management of change must embrace development of a school's culture if improvement is to be consistent and long-lasting.

David Hargreaves (1999) has mapped out a clear and persuasive route for practitioners to explore the school's culture. Noting that not much is yet known about the characteristics of effective school cultures, he argues that three core capabilities underlie the culture of an effective school:

- a *monitoring* capability, or scanning the school's internal and external environment for pressures and problems, for opportunities and for partnerships. This capability provides the school with the skill of linking internal self-evaluation to external potentialities;
- a *proactive* capability, or having a can-do philosophy, relishing challenge, and so looking ahead positively, taking into account the long-term as well as the short-term view. This capability generates optimism and confidence;
- a *resource deployment* capability, auditing the full range of the school's resources (human and intellectual as well as material and financial) and directing them to the key purposes of schooling. This capability breeds goal achievement.

(p. 65)

Hargreaves also points out that school leaders often have difficulty in recognising that the core of school improvement is what goes on in classrooms, and that school cultures need to be transformed so that they empower and energise teachers to be better classroom teachers. When teachers advocate educational reform, as Seymour Sarason (1982) has pointed out, they are rarely referring to what they can or should do in their own classrooms. So what can be done about classroom teaching and learning?

Focus on teaching and learning

Even if they do not envisage change, teachers often welcome a proposal to emphasise questions of teaching and learning, as they think these are at the heart of their professional activities. Yet debates in schools about how to give priority to teaching and learning are often confused and inconclusive. There are various reasons for this. The National Curriculum has greatly reduced teachers' discretion in *what* to teach. A substantial area of professional judgement has thus been removed. In

America, and in some parts of Europe, how you teach a subject is also externally pre-determined through choice of textbook or mandated teaching schemes. In the UK strong external pressure has recently been put on teachers to teach in a particular way (e.g. in setted rather than mixed-attainment groups, whole-class teaching rather than individual or group learning).

The National Literacy Strategy is often claimed to reflect an increasing distrust of teachers' professional judgement. At its worst, external pressure is based on a belief that there is one 'right' way to teach a particular topic or skill to a particular group of pupils. Proponents of this belief are often faced with what one of my colleagues calls 'the infuriating success of the wrong teaching methods'. There has also been a preoccupation with teacher performance, rather than with successful student learning. It is very important, of course, that the quality of teaching in any school is of the highest possible standard. But there is an increasing danger that teachers (and inspectors) will assume that a performance which satisfies the relevant criteria for the quality of teaching will necessarily bring with it a proportionate increase in students' learning. We should also be wary of the widespread belief that frequent assessment of students' learning, followed by dissemination of the data so collected, will of themselves improve students' levels of attainment. Another problem is the territorial aspect of many schools' cultures which assumes a teacher's right to privacy in her/his own classroom, or at best reluctantly to receive visiting adults as 'intruders' who, it is thought, must be there to monitor teacher performance – unless, of course, they are there to support individual pupils with special educational needs. Teachers are also desperately short of time, and sometimes confidence or competence, to collect evidence about the nature and extent of pupils' learning and to relate such evidence to the quality of teaching involved.

Systematic professional development of teachers

There has developed a tradition, built up over many years, that courses organised away from the school site, and attended often only by one teacher from an individual school, are the main vehicle for the professional development of staff in matters of teaching and learning. The capacity of the school itself to explore such issues on site has been grossly underused. Finally, there have been few attempts to find evidence of the effect which the professional development of teachers might have on the quality of pupils' learning. This is a difficult task, not least because such a link has often been assumed rather than accurately tracked. There is encouragement in the findings of Greenwald *et al.* (1996) who report the pupil achievement gains associated with four possible investments of marginal resources. (see Figure 5.3).

The last three factors were much more closely associated with gains in pupils' achievement, with 'better educated and trained teachers' the most closely associated of all.

Linda Darling-Hammond (1997) has argued convincingly that if we want all children to learn in school, we need to understand how to teach in ways that respond to students' diverse approaches to learning, that are organised to take advantage of students' unique starting points, and that carefully scaffold work aimed at more proficient performances. Of course, it is important also to understand what schools must do to organise themselves to support teaching and learning, and to become themselves what Peter Senge (1990) calls 'learning organisations'. Leithwood and Louis (1998) provide an excellent and up-to-date overview of organisational learning in schools.

Teachers who doubt the potency of a focus on teaching and learning

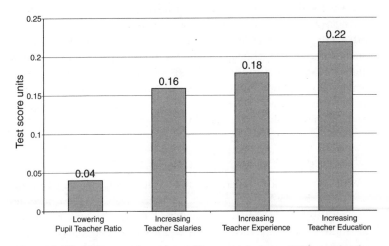

Figure 5.3 Size of increase in student achievement for every $500 spent on four areas (Greenwald *et al.* 1996)

may be reassured by evidence from *Inside the Black Box* by Paul Black and Dylan Wiliam (1998). Their pamphlet shows unequivocally that formative assessment of students' work raises standards, and that a good deal is known about how to improve formative assessment, particularly by involving students themselves in the process. When there are so many critiques of educational research which suggest that most of it is not relevant to classroom practice, it is vital that something so central to the teaching and learning process as formative assessment be widely understood and incorporated into professional practice.

More generally, we are at an exciting stage of uncovering more about how we learn, particularly from research on the brain (McNeil 1999), and how our emotional growth influences learning (Goleman 1996). Teachers are increasingly in a position to understand the processes of learning, and to choose their teaching approaches accordingly

Stoll and Fink (1996) suggest four types of professional development activity which ensure a focus on teaching and learning and on whole-school improvement:

1. Reflective research and study

Elliott (1991) has set out principles and procedures for teachers doing their own action research rooted in classroom or other school-based issues. Frost (1997) has developed these ideas, and matched the processes with accredited courses for teachers in a range of school development topics. Teachers cooperate in school-based groups, led by a tutor from a Higher Education Institution. There are obvious opportunities to develop these groups into district or LEA networks, and, using electronic media, into a national or international forum. In describing the competencies which teachers should develop for teaching in the twenty-first century, Gerald Grace (1999) includes:

> theoretical, self-evaluation and research competences. Teachers must have theoretical knowledge to inform, guide and give larger meaning to the classroom work they perform. Teachers must have the capacity to self-evaluate the quality of their work and not merely submit to external state inspection. They must have the capacity to research their own institutions and leading issues in education so that research does not remain the province of external 'experts'.

Professional development of staff based on the collegiate search for evidence about teaching and learning remains at the heart of school improvement.

The DfEE's recent paper (2000) *Professional Development: Support for Teaching and Learning* is very helpful in its insistence on seeing the school, and particularly the classroom, as the base for professional development. The document approvingly quotes American research which confirms that good professional development is generally school or classroom based, relates directly to what teachers are doing in their schools or classrooms, is often teacher-directed, and focuses intensely on assisting teachers to understand deeply the subject(s) they are teaching.

More generally, the DfEE paper prepared the way for professional development to become a much more routine part of teachers' professional lives, and to become the entitlement of all teachers. The implications of this are radical, as Joyce *et al.* (1997) point out:

> The core of educational modernisation will depend on the development of a completely different work place for teachers, one where teaching and curriculum are studied continuously, student learning is studied intensively, and the whole staff work cohesively to make initiatives to improve the school. All initiatives will founder, though, unless the workplace is changed radically so that time is built in to every week for study and development – not just preparation by individuals for specific lessons – but for collective mastery of new teaching strategies and the development of new curriculum plans. We urge policy-makers to instigate a kind of restructuring that creates time for collegial study and decision making, and ensures that what has been called 'staff development' becomes a regular and ongoing feature of every school. There is a burgeoning knowledge base about school improvement . . . as far as we can tell, the collegial study of teaching has been at the core of every documented successful initiative.

2. *Monitoring and coaching relationships*

The traditions of monitoring in the UK and coaching in the US are important ones, not least because they open up classrooms to professional visitors. Joyce (1991) has made a helpful distinction between '*workshop*', where new skills are learnt and practised, and '*workplace*' where new skills are applied. There is no reason, of course, why these two sites should not both be in the same school. Joyce and Showers (1982) found that incorporation of a new skill into a teacher's regular repertoire is most likely to be sustained when teachers observe each other in classrooms and provide accurate, specific and non-evaluative feedback. Constructive as such approaches are, the danger is that the focus becomes teacher performance rather than pupils' learning. These activities should be complemented by frequent cooperative studies of pupils' learning, using samples or portfolios of pupils' work across the curriculum, as well as quantitative and qualitative data based on regular and varied assessment methods.

I am also uneasy about the word 'monitoring'. It suggests 'checking for compliance', which is a static and potentially disabling process. Classroom observation, whether of students' learning or teacher performance, should be a much more dynamic process, with an expectation that both observer and observed will learn from the experience and put that learning to good professional use in their respective roles.

3. Appraisal

Bollington *et al.* (1990) have drawn attention to the link between appraisal and school development. In contrast to other forms of professional development concerned with improving students' learning, appraisal is the process where the professional strengths and weaknesses of the individual teacher should be the primary focus of the activity.

It is too early to assess what effect on appraisal the Government's new legislation on performance management will have. Within the welter of recent national initiatives, appraisal had slipped down the priority list in many schools, and performance management should certainly assure the regular assessment of teachers' performance, with the accompanying opportunity for professional discussion with their team leader about their work and their professional development. The link between performance management and pay is more complex and controversial, and its effects on students' standards of achievement less easy to predict. What is certain is that for the immediate future performance management will be near the top in most schools' agenda.

4. *Developing understanding and skills of the change process*

Fullan (1992) has emphasised that all successful school improvement involves an understanding of the processes of change at the levels of classroom and school practice, and awareness of the three phases involved in change: *initiation, implementation* and *institutionalisation*. Within the current professional climate it might be sensible to add a fourth phase to Fullan's list: *evaluation*. The importance of teachers' attitudes and values in preparing themselves better for change should not be underestimated, and Fullan's 'assumptions of change' (1991) are often very helpful to explore when working with teachers apprehensive about change.

The link between teachers' professional development and raising standards of pupil achievement remains a high priority for further research and debate by academics and practitioners. It is now, rightly, the first criterion in the TTA's list when considering bids for funding of teachers' in-service training. We still need more evidence to back up Barth's (1990) powerful advocacy:

> Probably nothing in a school has more impact on students in terms of skills development, self-confidence, or classroom behaviour than the personal and professional growth of their teachers.

Such growth needs the backing of the school, which should see itself as a learning community, with its head-teacher as the 'lead learner'. Fullan and Hargreaves (1992) offer teachers twelve guidelines in building a school culture of 'interactive professionalism':

- locate, listen to and articulate your inner voice;
- practise reflection in action, on action and about action;
- develop a risk-taking mentality;
- trust processes as well as people;
- appreciate the total person in working with others;
- commit to working with colleagues;
- seek variety and avoid 'balkanisation';
- redefine your role to extend beyond the classroom;
- balance work and life;
- push and support heads and other administrators to develop interactive professionalism;

- commit to continuous improvement and perpetual learning;
- monitor and strengthen the connection between your development and students' development.

(p. 86)

They also warn that these guidelines will not be effective in isolation from each other. However, the results of practising all twelve guidelines will be cumulative and contagious. Once mobilised, they will contribute to more fundamental and effective change than other existing reform strategies do.

There are other important aspects in the growth of 'professional learning communities', defined by their two key activities: *continuous enquiry* and *continuous improvement*. Rosenholtz (1989) found that teachers who felt supported in their own ongoing learning and classroom practice were more committed and effective than those who did not. She also found that teachers with a strong sense of their own efficacy were more likely to adopt new classroom behaviours, and that a strong sense of efficacy encouraged teachers to stay in the profession.

Another powerful form of teacher learning comes from networks of professional community that extend beyond the individual school. Such networks engage individuals in other professional contexts, and provide structured opportunities for teachers to reflect critically on their own practice, learn from and teach others, and through observation and discussion formulate new knowledge and ideas about teaching and learning (Hughes 2000; Darling-Hammond and McLaughlin 1995). An outward-looking approach like this also militates against two dangers described by Richard Elmore (1995): first, that the more militant advocates of change within a school isolate themselves from those least likely to embrace change. They thus create a social barrier between the two groups and 'virtually guarantee that the former will not grow in number and the latter will continue to believe that exemplary teaching requires extraordinary resources in an exceptional environment' (p. 17). Second, that such a group will behave increasingly like true believers in a particular version of the faith and become increasingly isolated from public scrutiny and discourse. In so doing, they also become increasingly vulnerable to attack from both reactionary colleagues and others outside the professional community.

Finally, implied in many of the descriptions of 'professional community' but rarely explicit, is the glue which binds many of the elements of any community together: trust. Leaders and their colleagues need over a period of time to build trust. In longitudinal and ongoing work in Chicago, Tony Bryk (2001) is discovering that 'relational trust' within the educational community is one of the key aspects of school improvement.

School improvement and inspection

The conditions under which schools make progress and improve the learning outcomes of their pupils are clearly and consistently laid out in research described earlier in this chapter. What evidence is there that current OFSTED inspection arrangements contribute to the process of school improvement, as is their stated purpose?

As has been already noted in Chapter 4, OFSTED itself obviously believes that the inspection process helps schools in difficulty to improve, although Riley (1998) found no evidence to support OFSTED's claim. As far as the majority of schools is concerned, the evidence, as one might expect, is both mixed and restricted. It is not easy to separate the effects of inspection from all the other external and internal factors which contribute to a school's improvement or deterioration. There has been too short a period since the beginning of OFSTED inspections to draw firm conclusions abut the medium or long-term effects of inspection.

In a survey of GCSE examination results over a four-year period achieved by a representative sample of pupils, Cullingford and Daniels (1999) found that pupils were less likely to achieve five or more high-grade GCSEs in years in which their schools are inspected.

> Generally, the proportion of pupils obtaining 5+ A–C grades appears to be increasing year on year. However, associated with OFSTED inspections, a slower rate of increase was observed . . . whatever the inspection period (within the year), OFSTED has a negative effect on the percentage of pupils successful in gaining higher grades. Putting it more bluntly, OFSTED inspections have the opposite effect to that intended. Year on year they lower standards.
>
> (p. 66)

TES 14 May 1999

Why inspections set you free

PLATFORM

Schools capable of managing
their own affairs should be
free to discount OFSTED
advice. To argue otherwise
would undermine their
independence, says chief
inspector Chris Woodhead

Lonsdale and Parsons (1998) also found a predominantly negative
picture of inspection's effect on school improvement. In their survey of
five schools after OFSTED inspection, they found wide variation in the
perceptions of OFSTED held by governors, teachers, head-teachers
and senior managers. Overall they conclude:

> In the vast majority of schools which are successful, OFSTED
> has caused considerable disruption to the normal life of the
> school. In the lead-up, during it and afterwards the effect of the
> inspection upon staff and pupils has been dramatic. In many
> cases it has disrupted the day-to-day routines of the school, the
> long-term planning process and the process of assessment and
> evaluation. The result has been to produce bland and superficial
> reports invariably making statements about collective worship,
> about differentiation and generalised issues that most teachers in
> the school could probably have highlighted. Major deficiencies
> in schools were missed by the inspection team while they
> reported issues that were common to almost all schools. In a
> time of shortage of resources (or at any time), should money be
> spent on a process that causes as much disruption as benefit? . . .
> The present process is subjugating, demeaning and deprofes-
> sionalising.

As was noted earlier in the book, the most comprehensive surveys of
inspection's effects on school improvement are these described by

Ouston and Davies (1998), the Brunel study (1999), and Scanlon (1999). Ouston and Davies report that OFSTED inspection clearly had encouraged development in practice in many of the schools taking part in the research, but that its effects were patchy and very dependent on both school and inspection team. They conclude that OFSTED inspection did have a positive impact on many schools, but that questions remain about whether there could be other, more effective and less costly ways of helping schools to improve their practice and outcomes. Schools which reported the maximum benefit from inspection were those which:

- maintained a professional confidence and did not allow the inspection to intimidate them;
- established a good relationship with the Registered Inspector;
- understood about the twin purposes of OFSTED: accountability and development;
- ensured that they met the accountability criteria;
- used OFSTED inspection as an audit of the school;
- used the opportunity to improve practice without creating excessive stress for teachers;
- noted poor inspection practice and brought it to the attention of the RgI;
- challenged the report if it was inaccurate;
- were realistic in deciding what should be done as a consequence of inspection;
- made informed and strategic choices about action to be taken;
- integrated plans resulting from the inspection with their previous plans;
- used the OFSTED report as a lever for change within the school and outside;
- assessed what was feasible; and
- made professional judgements about what was right for their school at that time.

(Ouston and Davies 1998)

Evidence about the impact of OFSTED inspection on the medium or long-term capacity of schools to improve is mixed. Margaret Scanlon (1999) found interesting differences between the perceptions of heads

Table 5.1 Effects of the inspection process

		Schools on special measures		Schools not on special measures	
		Heads (%)	Teachers (%)	Heads (%)	Teachers (%)
Staff morale	Improved	50	25	17	11
	No change	11	9	40	36
	Deteriorated	32	58	36	48
	Unable to say	2	5	3	3
	No response	5	4	4	3
School's reputation in the community	Improved	41	30	35	28
	No change	24	25	51	51
	Deteriorated	26	35	7	10
	Unable to say	6	9	4	7
	No response	3	2	3	4
School's ability to recruit staff	Improved	17	–	9	–
	No change	36	–	73	–
	Deteriorated	36	–	9	–
	Unable to say	8	–	5	–
	No response	3	–	4	–
School's ability to retain staff	Improved	21	–	5	–
	No change	46	–	80	–
	Deteriorated	24	–	7	–
	Unable to say	7	–	4	–
	No response	3	–	4	–
N		173	294	255	442

Note: Because percentages are rounded to the nearest integer, they may not sum to 100 in all cases.

and those of teachers, and between schools judged to require special measures and those not (see Table 5.1).

In very general terms, she reported that none of the respondents in the NFER survey (both heads and teachers) opposed school inspection as such, but objected to OFSTED because it seemed to create as many problems as it solved. Many favoured an inspection system that would provide more than a 'snapshot' view of the school, viewing the present system as unnecessarily stressful and giving an unrealistic picture of the school. They believed there should be greater advisory and supportive elements in the process, and that self-evaluation should play a greater part. Many also advocated an inspection system which set out to prevent rather than cure, with support being available from the LEA before rather than after inspection.

The essential tension remains: who is best placed to judge the quality of a school's provision? Those inside the school, or visitors from outside? and how can the judgements of both groups be harnessed to be of most value to a school? I believe that the two approaches are complementary, and will try in the next chapter to suggest a combined process which acknowledges the strengths and weaknesses of each individual element. A former Senior Chief Inspector, Sheila Browne (1979) should have the last word:

> However frequent their visits, HMI have always had to remember that their selective observation can never match the collective knowledge of the head and teachers; it is they, after all, who day by day with their pupils are and make a school or college. . . . A full inspection report is never the last word.

(p. 37)

QUESTIONS FOR FURTHER EXPLORATION

1   How can the contexts of school effectiveness and school improvement help in evaluating the potential contribution which school inspection might make to helping schools improve?

2   What are the most effective processes *inside* a school which promote improvement? What are the most effective contributions from *outside*?

3   What are the 'key factors' in helping schools improve?

4   If improving the quality of learning and teaching were to become a school's top priority, what changes in the culture of the school would you expect to see:

   (a) in the classroom?
   (b) around the school?
   (c) in teachers' attitudes and behaviour?
   (d) in senior managers' attitudes and behaviour?
   (e) in other aspects of school life?

5   What are the key aspects of staff development policy and practice to get right if schools are to improve?

6 What kind of inspection system would help raise standards?

This chapter draws on the evidence included in previous chapters on what helps schools improve. It explores developments in school evaluation in other parts of the world, as well as reviewing the concept of 'accountability'. Towards the end it outlines the framework for a system of school inspection which builds on most effective practice elsewhere, and which matches the needs of schools, LEAs and central government.

The next child, a small boy with a crown of close-cropped black hair and large pale eyes between almost colourless lashes, was an excellent reader too. He read from his book with grim determination in a loud and confident voice.

'You're a very good reader,' I commented when he snapped the book shut.

'Aye,' he replied nodding sagely.

'Do you like reading?'

'I do.'

'And I see from your reading card you've read a lot of books this year.'

'I have.'

'Do you read at home?'

'Sometimes.'

It was like extracting blood from a stone but I persevered.

'And what do you like reading about?' I asked cheerfully.

'Animals mostly.'

'Farm animals? Wild animals?'

'All animals.'

'And do you have any animals at home?'

'A few.'

'What sort?' I asked.

'Mostly black and white on green.'

'Pardon?'

'Cows,' he said quietly. 'I live on a farm.' Then a slight smile came to his lips and his expression took on that of the expert in the presence of an ignoramus – a sort of patient, sympathetic, tolerant look.

'Do you know owt about cows then?' he asked.

'No,' I said feebly. I should have left it there but I persisted. *'What would you like to tell me about the cows on your farm?'*

'There's not that much to tell really, cows is cows.'

'You're not a very talkative little boy, are you?' I said peering into the pale eyes.

'If I've got owt to say I says it, and I've got owt to ask I asks it,' he replied casually.

> (From *The Other Side of the Dale* by Gervase Phinn, Penguin, London, 1999)

Recent changes in OFSTED arrangements

What arrangements for inspection are likely to support schools in their efforts to raise standards?

The format of inspection procedures changes constantly. From January 2000, OFSTED introduced short inspections for 'the most effective schools', while retaining full inspections within a six year cycle for others. The four factors which may determine a short inspection are:

- a favourable report from the last inspection;
- a record of improvement (or sustained high standards);
- favourable achievements in relation to similar schools;
- good overall performance in relation to national average.

Other changes are now in place, too: a reduction in the period of notice of inspection, an acknowledgement of performance management in schools, a greater emphasis on educational inclusion,

recognition of the principles of 'Best Value' and a requirement to improve further the quality of inspection and standards of reports.

> Searching inspections and clear, well-written reports provide those who manage and those who teach in schools with an objective endorsement of the strengths of the school and a diagnosis of areas for improvement. Good inspections evaluate how good the school is and explain why it is as it is. Inspection by itself cannot raise standards; only those who work in schools can do that. But inspection is a potent catalyst for improvement.

(OFSTED 2000a)

Inspecting Schools: the Framework offers a reasonable justification for an inspection system, but there is little within the Framework or accompanying Inspection Handbooks to suggest that the Government or OFSTED have moved towards a system of school evaluation which will be more effective in raising the standards of all schools. It is still hard to agree with Michael Barber's comment, quoted on the back of the new Framework, that the previous Framework was very strongly based on education research, on school effectiveness and school improvement.

How, then, might a system of school evaluation, which involves both school self-evaluation and elements of external inspection, be constructed in order to give the highest priority to raising standards?

Central government, LEA and school

It would be foolish to argue simply for a return to pre-OFSTED times. The central relationships between central government, local authorities and individual schools have radically changed in the last twenty years, and new school inspection arrangements need to take this into account. There has been, in particular, a further reduction in the scope of local government responsibility generally, brought about principally by the mechanism of 'market forces', so that public service is being replaced as the dominant organising concept for educational provision by competitive self-interest and entrepreneurism. Local government is typically portrayed in the media as inefficient, stultifying and partisan, whereas the market, it is claimed, reinforces or requires the virtues of effort,

thrift, honesty, self-reliance, independence and risk-taking (Radnor and Ball 1996).

These changes imply new roles for the partners which are being hotly debated (see, for example, James Tooley (2000) and John Bangs (1998). The necessary adjustments were set out clearly by Cordingley and Kogan (1993):

> Market style systems will require a redefinition of professionalism in which professionals must take account of their clients' wishes, and empower both clients and providers to make choices. They must move with confidence through new governing arrangements and at the same time make creative contributions to the substance of education. Teachers who used to control their own curriculum have no input to the national curriculum. The drive towards external inspection weakens the opportunities for self-deployment through self-evaluation.

So one of the key tasks the new-style LEA must take on is a sharp and consistent impetus towards school improvement which is based on the collegiate study of effective teaching and learning. Cordingley and Kogan also reported that most of those interviewed in their study believed that local (or other intermediary) authorities should be democratically accountable to *elected* members rather than to *appointed* members.

The number of LEAs found by OFSTED to be performing inadequately continues to rise. LEAs now have specific and tough responsibilities towards schools judged by OFSTED to require special measures or to have serious weaknesses. As Levacic (1999) points out,

> LEAs are required to support schools with serious weaknesses and ensure that they improve within a year. . . . The latest legislation (School Standards and Framework Act, 1998) ensures that LEAs now function to implement central government education policy, which can be detailed and prescriptive. . . . LEAs are part of the government's structure for managing schools' performance and holding them accountable. If LEAs fail in these duties then, as the Secretary of State has made clear, he will look to replace them with private sector providers.

Although the arrangements for private sector providers to take over some or all LEA functions in 'failing' LEAs are now in place, it is far too early to judge their success in raising standards. LEAs are now being encouraged to make more use of providers, approved by the DfEE, *before* OFSTED inspections.

Core elements of a new inspection system

I have tried to suggest in this book that the current practice of OFSTED is out of step with the great tradition of English school inspection, and is too rigid and unreliable to meet the needs of schools in the twenty-first century. Calvinists might argue for the benefits of learning through pain if, in return for the suffering, the procedures provided a valid picture of a school's performance, or fulfilled their essential purpose of school improvement. But many inspectors know that schools are driven, in Matthew Arnold's words, to 'mechanical contrivances in which the teacher will and must more and more learn how to beat us'; that the 'snapshot' of the school takes precedence over constructive and considered advice about how to improve; that the whole-school, mechanical and inflexible model of school inspection – even with the 'light-touch', short inspections introduced in January 2000 – is not the most cost-effective way of raising standards in schools; and that those who work in schools should have the principal responsibility of evaluating their own performance, should be encouraged to regain confidence in their own professional judgements, and should be able to give an account of why such judgements were made. But citizens of the twenty-first century rightly require a wider accountability to both locally and nationally elected democratic assemblies. Each of the three main partners throughout the history of schooling (government, local authority and school), together with other stakeholders such as the Church (where this is relevant), governing bodies, students, teachers and parents, all have an important role to fulfil if inspection is to be as effective as it should be.

In outlining developments in the history of school inspection, I have pointed out several related issues which recur throughout the commentary. These are summarised (below) as a proposed framework of requirements for evaluating schools in the twenty-first century.

The core elements are:

- an inspection process which satisfies external accountability requirements at the same time as directly and vigorously promoting school improvement in individual schools;
- a consistent framework for the evaluation of schools which provides a flexibility in order to take into account the needs, circumstances, strengths and weaknesses of the individual school and its socio-economic setting;
- clear, complementary roles in inspection for those who have statutory responsibilities to provide an education service: central government, the local education authority, and the individual school;
- the collection of evidence which provides as detailed, honest and 'typical' a portrait of the school as possible;
- the complementary evidence of the intimate knowledge of a school held by those who work there, permanently and intermittently, and of the different perspectives of professional experience elsewhere. The relationship between 'insiders' and 'outsiders' is a dynamic one, with each group learning from the other;
- mechanisms of support and intervention which are in place for schools which, whatever the blend of internal and external reasons, are getting into difficulty, and these mechanisms are brought into play before those difficulties become a crisis;
- a national system which makes it plain to the public the degree to which an individual school is responsible for its own strengths or weakness, and the degree to which it benefits or suffers from local or national circumstances or policies;
- flexibility within the process to review, and if necessary support, specific elements of a school's provision rather than assuming a full school evaluation is necessary;
- An inspection system which invites contributions from 'key stakeholders' in the process of education, and gives their evidence appropriate value in the formulation of judgements about the quality of process;
- recognition that the reliable formation of such judgements is often a complex and tentative process, in which all participants acknowledge their capacity to learn more. Training in the skills

of evaluation is continuously available to those working in the education service. (Such training is very different from OFSTED's definition, which is little more than familiarisation with 'the Framework';

- a continuing effort to convince those working inside and outside schools (including politicians) that an external inspection is not *per se* more rigorous, more valid and more reliable than systematic and consistent supported self-evaluation;
- agreement that the 'internal' and 'external' aspects of school evaluation are not seen as exclusive or competitive but complementary processes which provide mutual support to schools seeking to raise the standards of their pupils' achievement.

These are the essential issues which need to be resolved in developing an inspection system which will promote school improvement. There is virtually common ground amongst those working in education that a future inspection system requires two elements: the *internal*, and the *external*.

David Hargreaves (1995a) believes that internal self-evaluation of a school on its own is inadequate:

A school's internal audit or self-evaluation . . . looks an amateur enterprise. The teachers are not trained in the skills of inspecting and auditing; they lack a wider perspective and are inclined to parochialism; their criteria for defining strengths and weaknesses are more likely to be implicit and closed; strongly identified with their school, they cannot guarantee detachment in their judgements; any strengths they proclaim may be pure rhetoric; governors and parents would be foolish to take all they say at face value.

(p. 117)

Michael Barber (1996) too, argues that both internal and external perspectives are necessary in school evaluation.

Internal and external evaluation

There are various models for internal evaluation. OFSTED's *Framework* and *School Evaluation Matters* have provided a basic and respected model, and schools, LEAs and other agencies have developed self-evaluation frameworks which are different from the basic models in ways which match local requirements and priorities. Some of these have been described in outline in Chapter 3, and are discussed in detail in the book by John MacBeath in this series.

But what of the relationship between internal school self-evaluation and teachers' accountability?

Accountability

In seeking to define 'accountability', various writers (e.g. Bush 1980) identify three aspects: *moral accountability*, through which one is answerable to one's clients; *contractual responsibility*, through which one is accountable to one's employers and political masters; and *professional accountability*, through which one is responsible to oneself and to one's colleagues. Eraut (1992) goes on to define 'professional' accountability as including:

- a moral commitment to serve the interests of clients;
- a professional obligation to self-monitor and periodically to review the effectiveness of one's practice;
- a professional obligation to expand one's repertoire, to reflect on one's experience, and to develop one's expertise;
- an obligation that is professional as well as contractual to contribute to the quality of one's organisation;
- an obligation to reflect on and contribute to discussions on the changing role of one's profession in a wider society.

While this seems to be an admirable and constructive definition, it reflects processes which are currently not often available to classroom teachers. Lack of time and resources are no doubt the main reasons for this, but there is also evidence of a widespread shift of perceived accountability from teachers themselves to external agencies in the new public management of education (Bottery and Wright 1999). The current emphasis on standards in the UK may also be undermining the capacity and confidence of teachers to give a logical 'account' of their practice to themselves, other teachers and the various groups to whom they are accountable (Reed and Learmonth 2000). Teachers need to feel some sense of personal commitment to a system of accountability if it is to be effective in securing improvement. As we have seen in Chapter 5, research in the UK and USA makes it clear that school improvement depends on the commitment and consistent professional development of teachers, working together both within and across schools, in order to improve the quality of teaching and learning and thus raise standards. The national standards produced by the TTA reflect a welcome start in entitling, perhaps requiring, teachers to be involved in a continuous programme of professional development which will increase their capacity to give a rigorous and systematic account of their work. The Best Practice Research Scholarships, which started in September 2000, are another hopeful sign that classroom-based research by individual teachers, or by small groups, will become more widespread (Frost *et al.* 2000).

Linda Darling-Hammond (1997) points out that reliance on bureaucratic accountability cannot be reduced without strengthening professional accountability in its stead.

In the context of individual teachers, a definition of professional accountability might include the ability to give an 'account' of one's practice in the classroom. The account would reflect the capacity to

Daily Express 4 November 1998

TEACHERS 'NOT FIT TO JUDGE THEMSELVES'

TEACHERS are not capable of judging their own strengths and weaknesses, schools inspection chief, Chris Woodhead, told them yesterday.

Claims that schools should be able to evaluate their own performance without the external scrutiny of inspectors were "nonsensical", he told the think-tank Demos and the National Union of Teachers.

make well-considered choices from a wide repertoire of teaching and learning approaches, according to the topic and according to the learning needs of a specific group of pupils; to be able to provide evidence of the learning that did, or did not, take place in the lesson; and to decide, using such evidence in the context of previous experience, on future action. As all teachers develop their capacity to give an account, the process should promote within a school an increasing amount of knowledge about the progress and performance of students and, ultimately, about the school itself. It should help to shape, sustain and strengthen both the professional and public understanding of the essential business of schooling: teaching and learning. It should also contribute to the continuous improvement of professional practice in ways which promote schools as learning communities, and which advance the life-long learning of students and teachers alike.

Accounts of professional practice become part of an 'accountability system' when they are made available to groups (e.g. governing bodies, the LEA, a national inspection service, parents, the local community, the government) who are stakeholders in the success of the school. To sustain the accountability those groups must have the opportunity (not necessarily the duty) to scrutinise the accounts, and ask further questions or make suggestions for change. Teachers are bound to consider these responses, but also have the right to decide whether or how to adapt their practice.

In presenting an account of its performance, a school will probably review the proper balance on a wide range of issues. These include:

- does the school evaluate its success using test and examination results only, or does it include a wide range of other desirable student outcomes?
- how much time, and what priority, does it give to reporting to a range of audiences: the school itself, governing body, LEA, OFSTED, parents, etc?
- what are the 'units of responsibility' within a school's system? What about the difference in performance between subject departments in secondary schools, or year teams in primary schools?
- what is the right balance in the system between support and pressure? Between autonomy and compliance?
- does the school go for short-term improvement which is visible in

test-scores, or opt for longer-term improvement in students' skills which may or may not be visible during their time at school?

- is the school judged on the progress of individual students within the institution, or as a whole school against a background of national data?
- within the framework of the National Curriculum, *what* is to be learnt, and *how* is it to be learnt?
- if time and energy are limited, how are self-review and the promotion of improvement to be reconciled?
- perhaps most difficult of all, how should a school balance the account of its *processes* with that of its *outcomes*?

A risk inherent in this perspective on professional accountability is that the development of professional accountability within the individual school is bound to be restricted, however effective the school. In poorly performing schools, the process is likely to be incoherent and inconsistent; at worst, schools may simply recycle existing inadequacies. So how can heads and teachers find out what is happening elsewhere?

OFSTED's current practice of recruiting 'Additional Inspectors' (AIs) from the ranks of existing heads and other senior staff is a start, although training in inspecting skills is minimal. Some schools, LEAs and other agencies in the UK are promoting opportunities for teachers to visit each other's schools with a planned programme of observation, discussion or report, rather than 'just to see what's going on' (Hughes 2000).

But there are also interesting examples of supported school self-evaluation around the world, all of which give teachers the opportunity to develop their professional accountability.

Supported school self-evaluation in other countries

In a wide-ranging account of practice worldwide, John MacBeath (1999) finds useful Trond Alvik's three categories of internal and external school evaluation:

- *Parallel.* Both school and external review body conduct their own evaluations. They may afterwards share and compare findings.

- *Sequential.* The school conducts its own evaluation and then the external body uses that as a basis for its review. This may work in the opposite direction. The external body furnishes the school with feedback or findings which they then work on.
- *Cooperative.* The two parties discuss and negotiate the process and different interests and viewpoints are taken into account simultaneously.

Examples of arrangements which seem particularly positive in the UK and elsewhere include these six: Scotland; USA; The Channel Islands; The Netherlands; Victoria, Australia; and London Borough of Wandsworth.

Scotland

Using Alvik's categories, the Scottish approach is an example of a system moving from the parallel mode to the sequential, with some hints of how a genuinely cooperative approach might develop.

From the appointment in 1840 of the first school inspector in Scotland, arrangements for inspection have proceeded broadly in line with those of England. But there are significant differences (Bone 1968).

School self-evaluation procedures have been given higher priority, and HM Inspectorate's function now include monitoring arrangements for quality assurance through the scrutiny of school and college performance carried out by the Inspectorate's Audit Unit, set up in 1992. The main tool for this activity is the positively entitled *How Good is our School? Self-evaluation using Performance Indicators*, developed by the Audit Unit in consultation with teachers and education authority officers. This process of self-evaluation is one element of what the Scots call a 'quality culture' in education:

> external assessment provided by HMI would be complemented by schools undertaking systematic self-assessment, development planning and reporting of performance to school boards, parents and the wider community, and by systematic monitoring of quality arrangements at local authority level.
>
> (McGlynn and Stalker 1995)

One of the most important elements within this process of self-evaluation is the collection of student views on the quality of educational provision. Many teachers, and some inspectors, were initially sceptical about the value of asking students to express their views, but 'the positive and insightful nature of students' comments continues to surprise schools seven years down the line' (MacBeath 1999).

With self-evaluation in place, only a sample of schools, including independent schools, is inspected annually. Arrangements for inspection are similar to those in England, but there are differences:

- the education authority, governing body, school board and parents are invited to give their views of a school prior to an inspection;
- a draft report of the outcome of the inspection is discussed with the head-teacher, the director of education or chairperson of the governors of an independent school, and the chairperson of the school board;
- the recommendations of the report provide an agenda, to be agreed by the school and the education authority, for a follow-up inspection within 12–18 months. The conclusions of the follow-up inspection are published in the form of a letter from the chief inspector to the director of education or the chairperson of governors;
- the range of inspections undertaken within an education authority is used to evaluate the work of the authority, and in particular, its approach to quality assurance;
- at the end of each inspection head-teachers and their staff are invited to complete a questionnaire giving their views about the inspection.

USA

Efforts to combine self-evaluation processes with some sort of external inspection are under way in the USA, although the word 'inspection' is not used: it is thought to be too frightening to teachers, and too hierarchical in its assumption that 'inspectors' will know all the answers in improving schools. The procedures developed by David Green in Chicago's 'School Change through Inquiry Project' (SCIP) and by Tom

Wilson and his colleagues in Rhode Island draw on the English inspection tradition. Each has interesting innovations from which our current system could learn.

The processes involved in SCIP place both internal and external reviewers in the role of 'enquirers', rather than the external reviewers as 'experts'. Green rightly emphasises that the crucial process of inquiry has as its core 'the capacity to know what you see, rather than to see only what you know'. In 'Quality Review', schemes originally developed by Green in New York and Illinois, teams of reviewers include representatives of the State Education Department, local principals of schools, and representatives of business and industry. All have had special training in the processes of review, which give priority to understanding three aspects of school life:

- teaching and learning;
- student learning, progress and achievement; and
- schools as learning communities.

The review process is itself a model for schools to develop as inquiring communities and involves schools in continuous self-review. The external school quality review occurs in a five-year cycle, followed by annual self-review conducted by the school itself. It gives practice, both to visiting reviewers and to teachers in the school being reviewed, in becoming 'faithful witnesses' during their inquiry.

Both the review process and self-review encourage honesty rather than 'show-casing'. The external reviewers may be in the school for a week, but the format encourages both reviewers and reviewed to set the school's performance in the context of time rather than seeing it as a 'snapshot' only. Apart from inquiry, the two other key processes involved in Green's work are first, the interrogation and discussion of the evidence gathered in order to arrive at an overall perspective agreed by the team; and second, the publication of the results of the inquiry so that they, along with the process itself, may be accessible to the critical scrutiny of a wider community.

Rhode Island educators also draw on the traditions of English inspection in assembling the different elements of Rhode Island's SALT scheme ('School Accountability for Learning and Teaching'). There are several activities in the SALT cycle:

- *Self-study* – these are focused inquiry activities that the school's own school improvement team conducts, concentrating on three 'focus' areas. These are: student learning; teaching; and the structures and processes within and outside the school that promote and support learning and teaching.
- *A school improvement plan* based on evidence gained during self-study, which requires the exercise of professional judgement in deciding what action should take place.
- *The school visit*, in which a team of practising Rhode Island teachers, a parent, a school administrator, school committee member, a member of a higher education institution, and a member of Rhode Island's Education Department conduct a four-day visit. Each school expects a visit every five years. The team of visitors writes a report on the school's performance in each of the three SALT focus areas, and makes recommendations for the school's development.
- A school '*compact for learning*' is then drawn up by school, district and State Department of Education. The purpose of this agreement is to ensure that the school has as much capacity as possible to implement its revised improvement plan. The compact specifies what the district and the department will do to support the school.
- *School report night* – schools report to their parents and community at least once a year on how well they are doing, their plans for improving results, and how the school community can help the school to address those challenges.

In both self-study and the visits, the priority given to lesson observation means that reviewers can 'weigh and consider the quality of actual practice'. Though self-study and the visit use many other ways of assessing schools – through test scores, programme evaluation, surveys of perceptions of the school's strengths and weaknesses, research based on social science methodology – Tom Wilson sees the visit as a *practitioner's* way of knowing and judging a school. It reflects

> passionate pursuit to increase their understanding of how their daily practice works and how they can improve it. That passion is the work of the professional. Furthermore, it earns public respect.

Wilson goes on to outline eight stages in the visit:

- the team's initial observations and perceptions; which guide the
- collection of evidence (no 'hearsay' allowed), and leads to
- drawing preliminary conclusions from the evidence;
- application of professional judgement by the team;
- team discussion and decision-making, which result in
- developing broadly-focused recommendations, based on the conclusions;
- commending areas of excellence, and
- writing the team report (written to persuade, rather than to prescribe).

The developing systems in Rhode Island, New York and Illinois are each tailored to meet the specific needs and requirements of their own local communities. But they have in common two elements from which we can learn: *practitioner accountability* and *relevant training*.

Each system is developing a *practitioner's accountability* which not only relates directly and powerfully to school improvement, but also reflects an appropriate acceptance of the need for external accountability to State requirements. Thomas Sobol, recently Commissioner of Education for New York State, who invited David Green to introduce School Quality Review into the state, comments on this definition of accountability:

> There's an analogy to the way the good teacher teaches a class. The good teacher does not organise and conduct the class so as best to prevent misbehaviour by the few – with a lot of strict, confining rules and an air of intimidation. The good teacher creates a climate in which young people can discover their talents and discipline them and express them. And then deals with problems by exception. That's the kind of accountability system we think is appropriate for the vast preponderance of schools in the state. It doesn't presume that someone in central authority knows exactly how things should be done and the rest of you have to shape up and do it that way. What it does is engage people at a professional and human level that attempts to bring out the best in them. When you have that kind of attitude and activity going on in a school, you're likely to get good practice.
>
> (Sobol, in Olson 1994)

Each system also provides *relevant training* for the members of reviewing teams, but also builds within the reviewing team and the reviewed school the capacity to develop new skills of evaluation. Thus one of the strengths of these American arrangements is that both in pre-training and in the process of the review, members of the reviewing team may develop skills of inspecting and auditing. They may acquire a wider perspective, may gain greater clarity and consistency in the criteria for defining strengths and weaknesses; and they may increase their capacity to develop detachment in their judgements. All the time team members are encouraged both to draw upon and increase their unique strength: their professional knowledge as practitioners. Evidence which increases that knowledge comes from classroom observation, from the analysis of data, from the 'shadowing' of students, from the exploration of student work, and from the carrying out of planned surveys and interviews with members of the school community. In short, the visit system is designed as an important dimension of the State's commitment to the professional development of teachers.

Most important of all, these procedures stress the role of the external reviewer and the reviewed as colleague 'learners'. In the common pursuit of an honest and useful evaluation of a school, the experience of other practitioners is imported to complement the intimate, long-term knowledge of the school being reviewed. External reviewer and classroom teacher are drawn into passionate questioning about how standards of teaching and learning may be improved, and each learns from the other. Such professional accountability avoids the dangers inherent in current OFSTED procedures and style which encourage teachers to comply with an externally-determined checklist. There is a real danger that teachers will find themselves adopting the values and language of external accountability mechanisms. Whatever their intentions, the processes of external audit may lead to declining standards of performance through a basic lack of trust and the undermining of professional staff autonomy.

For further accounts of American developments, see Ancess (1996) and Wilson (1996, 2000).

The Channel Islands

The Channel Islands have developed an interesting process which they call 'validated school self-evaluation'. Managed by a steering group comprising senior officers drawn from each island and other co-opted members, the scheme includes these key elements:

- *a framework for the development and review of schools* influenced by the OFSTED model, and agreed by representative working parties;
- *external evaluation of the whole scheme;*
- *funding is made available to schools* to support self-review, and to support the implementation of one or more of the key areas identified for action;
- *appropriate training for staff,* both for internal school self-evaluation and for the validation process;
- *a register of approved validators* – those eligible include officers and advisers in the Islands; heads and deputies; experienced heads of departments and subject coordinators; and OFSTED-trained inspectors.

One of the most important benefits of the Channel Islands scheme is the way in which teachers have the opportunity to develop evaluative skills in other schools, and at the same time exchange information or ideas about effective practice across the school system.

The Netherlands

An interesting element of school self-evaluation in The Netherlands is the influence of a higher education institution (the University of Twente) whose research work in school effectiveness is contributing to a 'sequential' system in which the school first conducts its own self-evaluation, and the role of external inspection is then to validate the quality of the school's internal procedures. The Netherlands chief inspector encourages a variety of approach to school evaluation; so there is no 'standard' framework of inspection.

Amongst a range of roles which The Netherlands' school inspectors are required to fulfil, there is an important responsibility both to offer advice to school staffs, and to coordinate the development of advice networks with a range of providers and local education authorities. Newly recruited inspectors must follow an intensive three month preparatory course and then undertake further systematic training activities every year thereafter. Inspectors have a responsibility for about 100 schools if primary specialists, about thirty if secondary. Schools are inspected annually, and an inspection lasts from between half a day to a whole day. An inspection of a school is carried out by the inspector responsible for it, thus guaranteeing that the evaluation is not carried out by 'a stranger' and that there is a continuing and constructive bond between school and inspector (Scheerens *et al.* 1998).

Victoria, Australia

The quality assurance system in Victoria has two purposes, reflecting the classic tension: to satisfy government requirements about accountability for the outcomes of schooling, and to support schools in their attempts to improve standards of student achievement.

The Victorian system is based on three premises:

- that external evaluation is more effective in improving school performance, when schools have well developed internal evaluation processes (Cuttance 1994);
- that school self-evaluation without some external component lacks the rigour necessary to effect real and lasting improvement in school performance (Victorian Commission of Audit 1993);
- that evaluation processes should assist schools not only to analyse their performance but also to improve the effectiveness and efficiency of their management practices. To this end, there is a significant emphasis in the accountability framework on management information systems, and on the analysis, as far as possible, of objective, quantitative data to evaluate quality in key areas of school operations (Davies 1990).

The three key elements in the accountability framework are the *school charter*, the *school annual report* and the *triennial school review*. They provide schools with a planning, monitoring, reporting and performance-review framework over a three year period.

Each of the processes is sponsored at school level by the school council and each contains an element of negotiated agreement between the Victorian Department of Education and the school. This is embodied in the school charter, which is a three-year performance agreement between the school and the Department. It is continued in the school's annual report, which contains performance data decided by the school as well as performance data required by the Department, and is fully expressed in the triennial school review, where the school conducts a self-assessment using the data in three annual reports. That self-assessment is verified by an external reviewer contracted to represent the Department. In the review, school and reviewer agree on specific directions for the school's next charter.

For quality assurance purposes, school reviewers are trained and accredited by the Office of Review prior to undertaking any verification work. All schools undertaking a review complete an evaluation, rating the performance of the reviewer, outlining their suggestions for improvements in the process and indicating their comments on the verification day and report.

The Office of Review conducts a detailed analysis of all verification reports to ensure that they fit within the guidelines, are compatible with Departmental policy and provide meaningful direction for the school in developing and implementing its improvement plans over the next three years. In addition, Office of Review staff act as observers of the performance of individual reviewers.

The role of the independent reviewer is thus critical in encouraging the school to set challenging goals and improvement priorities for the next three-year charter period.

For further details of the system in Victoria, see Ferguson *et al.* (2000).

London Borough of Wandsworth

Many LEAs in England include in their Education Development Plans arrangements for supporting individual schools in their self-evaluation. Some have developed their own self-evaluation frameworks in partnerships with schools, which usually include an evaluative element to assess the effectiveness of the procedures. Of these processes some are informal and flexible (e.g. Derbyshire's Quality Development Dialogue (CLEA 1997)), others are more formal and structured.

London Borough of Wandsworth has a well-established programme of Annual School Review (ASR). During the last few years schools have gradually, with inspectorate support, taken more responsibility for monitoring and evaluating their own practices and procedures. At this stage schools which demonstrate that they have sufficiently robust and reliable procedures to ensure that school improvement is taking place can apply for LEA accreditation of their self-review processes. The criteria for accredited school self-review (ASSRE) were agreed by a working party of heads and inspectors, keeping the OFSTED Framework in mind.

Criterion 1   Whole school improvement of educational standards

- Pupils' attainment and progress
- Attitudes, behaviour and personal development
- Attendance and punctuality

Criterion 2   Whole school improvement of educational provision

- The quality of teaching
- The effectiveness of the curriculum
- The effectiveness of assessment

Criterion 3   Management and leadership

- Management responsibility for standards achieved
- Management responsibility for the quality of education provided

For each of the three criteria, the school has to provide evidence for the LEA that appropriate processes are in place.

The role of LEAs

The LEA's task is to challenge schools to raise standards continuously and to apply pressure where they do not. That role is not one of control. Those days are gone. An effective LEA will challenge schools to improve themselves, being ready to intervene where there are problems, but not to interfere with those schools that are doing well. . . . The leadership function of an LEA . . . is about winning the trust and respect of schools and championing the value of education in its community.

(DfEE 1997)

The responsibility of the LEA to contribute to school improvement is one of its main roles, and is specifically the subject of LEA inspection by OFSTED. Although LEAs are explicitly required to anticipate and intervene in schools getting into difficulty, such a role implies careful monitoring of all schools to obtain a complete picture. There is also a strong case for LEAs having the responsibility to intervene if a school appears to be unable to sustain the quality of *part* of its provision – for example, early years provision in a primary school, or one department in a secondary school. The LEA has a continuing responsibility for the quality of its schools and is better placed than occasional visitors (like OFSTED inspectors) to 'know' the strengths and weaknesses of its schools. But, as Kenneth Baker pointed out in 1988:

> Experience in the past of variation of LEAs' capacity to perform adequately this monitoring function will require a 'safety net' to catch schools which, for whatever reason, are not being successfully supported by their LEA in providing an adequate standard of provision.

LEAs should not be required to limit their attention to 'failing' schools, or those at risk of becoming 'failing' schools. Nor should what Stoll and Fink (1996) call 'cruising schools – the unidentified ineffective school' be the only ones to be added, although there is certainly scope to look more searchingly at the performance of schools where average attainment levels of pupils on entry are high. The danger is that in following the DfEE's (1997) principle that LEAs should intervene in schools in inverse proportion to their success, LEAs become restricted in their view of the capabilities of all schools to improve, because so much of their day-to-day experience is with schools in difficulty. Through organising and through participating in the external reviews of *all* schools within their area, LEAs would both contribute long-standing and detailed knowledge, and gain further information about recent, present and future developments. LEA inspectors would be required in this role to make judgements about the performance of schools as well as to suggest options for making improvements in identified areas of weakness. This is a complex task, but not, as some commentators have argued, impossible or undesirable: we do, after all, expect all headteachers to perform the triple role of judging, challenging and supporting on a day-to-day basis in their school.

A future inspection system

The most coherent blueprint for a future inspection system in the UK has come from OFSTIN, a voluntary and unfunded group of educationists who have met since 1966 to keep the OFSTED system of inspection under review. On the basis of various conferences, seminars and the independent review published in 1999, OFSTIN conclude that there ought to be six basic changes to the current inspection system:

- replace the present unreliable private 'contracting' system with a professional, qualified and trained national inspectorate;
- give schools the responsibility for assessing their own performance and progress while inspectors monitor, and report on their success;
- require inspectors to discuss their judgements with teachers and to offer advice and assistance to schools as part of inspection;
- restore teachers' responsibility for deciding upon effective methods of teaching rather than being told how to teach by the inspectorate;
- spend much less taxpayers' money on inspecting schools and much more on helping them to improve themselves, ensuring that the inspection system provides value for money;
- make the national schools' inspectorate accountable to an independent body.

These proposals are certainly constructive and would make a substantial contribution to the improvement of the inspection system. There is no mention, however, of the LEA's role in a future inspection system, possibly because OFSTIN is unsure of the future of LEAs, or because the group was not agreed on the most appropriate role. So what are the roles which the three partners – central government, LEAs and the school – might play in a future inspection system?

:d role of a *national school inspectorate* is set out below:

- Providing professional advice to the Government of the day, both in formation of policy and in assessing the effects of policy.
- Monitoring the quality of school reviews and coordinating the collection of national data, quantitative and qualitative, about school evaluation and publishing regular reports in accessible formats.
- Monitoring and supporting LEAs' priorities within their Education Development Plans to promote school improvement. This monitoring role should include the right to intervene if LEA responsibilities are not being fulfilled.
- Inspection of important aspects of national provision which are not amenable to single institution evaluation, e.g. curriculum continuity between Key Stages 2 and 3, or the continuity of 3–19 educational provision within a particular community.
- Coordination of a programme of training to develop skills of school evaluation. This should have both a national and regional layer. Training would be available for those in various roles within the education service, and at all levels.
- Development of criteria for judging school performance which are sensitive to the benefits and challenges which different socio-economic communities provide.
- Contributing one national inspector to each school review (or to an agreed sample), so that information can flow in both directions between individual school and the centre.

The role of *an LEA* (or other regional agency) is ⌐

- The coordination and, ultimately, validation of sc⌐
  evaluation frameworks. These frameworks should be a⌐
  by elected members of the LEA who should also have reg⌐
  access to the information provided by the evaluations.
- In partnership with higher education institutions, providing
  training in school evaluation skills at the local level; and also
  promoting school-based action research relevant to school
  development.
- Monitoring standards of student achievement in the LEA
  schools, and having the power to intervene early if schools (or
  particular parts of school provision) are getting into difficulty.
- Coordination of the process of assembling local teams of professional inspectors and providing relevant and on-going
  training for such inspectors. Inspection teams should include
  members based in neighbouring LEAs, so that the experience
  and perspectives of all involved are extended.
- Contributing to the national database the quantitative and
  qualitative evidence from local professional visits.
- Supporting head-teacher and teacher appraisal in schools, and
  monitoring the distinction between school self-evaluation and
  performance management (i.e. sustaining the difference
  between assessing student learning and progress on the one
  hand, and appraising teacher performance on the other).

The role of a *school* is as follows:

- Developing and implementing self-evaluation frameworks, in cooperation with the LEA, which give opportunities to all stakeholders in the school community (teachers, non-teaching staff, governors, parents and students) to make constructive comments.
- Fostering both intra-school and inter-school networks for debate about professional practice by offering a clear purpose and specific learning tasks for these exchanges.
- Making available, in accessible form, regular reports to the local community about progress and problems in the school's performance. The validity of these reports would be confirmed by the LEA. If no agreement is possible, the nature of the disagreement would be included in the report.

Although I have set out the proposed elements of a new school quality assurance system in a way which separates national, local and individual school roles, the system presupposes that sort of partnership between the three agencies envisaged in the Education Reform Act of 1988 and in the Code of Practice on LEA-School Relations (DfEE 1999).

John Bangs (1998) has described the details of a new social partnership between schools and LEAs which takes account of recent Government initiatives such as Education Action Zones (EAZ) and Education Development Plans. As Bangs points out:

It matters little to classroom teachers where external services they need come from so long as they are effective. It does matter, however, to classroom teachers if they are isolated professionally from their colleagues in other schools; if they are entirely dependent on the services being purchased by the Head and the governing body, and if the school organisation framework prevents them from being involved in the professional community. LEAs now have the opportunity to demonstrate that they can add value to the professional lives of teachers.

Whatever the organisational arrangements, it is clear the 'the culture' of inspection will also have to change. Validated school self-evaluation will have to prove itself as a more rigorous and reliable judgement of a school's performance than the arbitrary 'snapshot' which Chris Woodhead says OFSTED currently offers. The considered judgement of those who know a school well, whether in the school itself or in its LEA, will be trusted, rather than that of the hastily-assembled group of outsiders, many of whom will not know each other and who are likely to have no previous or further contact with the school after an OFSTED inspection. Crucially, those working in schools – who, OFSTED notes, are the only people who can raise standards – will reclaim the responsibility for reviewing a school's performance. They will be required to rebuild their competence and confidence in their own judgements about learning and teaching approaches, through which the levels of their students' achievements can be raised. They will welcome, and grow to expect and trust, experience from other schools and other areas of the country, reflected in the membership and collective judgements of visiting inspection teams. Experience in Scotland and the USA shows that the judgements of such visiting teams proposed in this book may be just as 'unvarnished and literal' (to quote Matthew Arnold's words) as those of current OFSTED inspectors, and may be more acceptable to the schools concerned because of the methodology and composition of the teams involved.

QUESTIONS FOR FURTHER EXPLORATION

1   What does 'accountability' mean to you? What do you think of the concept of 'practitioner accountability' developed in this chapter?

2   Reviewing school evaluation procedures from other countries, what would you include, and what would you leave out, in inspection arrangements for the twenty-first century?

3   What is your ideal balance between national, local and school responsibilities in school inspection arrangements?

4   Which aspects of inspection arrangements in this chapter do you welcome, and which do you reject?

5   In the final analysis, what's in it for schools?

7 Conclusion: what's in it for schools?

The proposed inspection arrangements outlined in the last chapter give the highest priority to supporting schools in their efforts to raise standards. There are clear and interdependent roles for agencies at each of three levels: national, local and individual school. The complexity of 'knowing a school' is recognised by the inclusion in the inspection team of members with knowledge of the recent history and contemporary circumstances of the school. There will also be a national inspector who will bring to the school a broader perspective and be an important link in a chain of accountability. Safeguards within the system give clear responsibilities to LEAs to act early and decisively in the case of schools in difficulty, with the safety-net of national intervention if local efforts are inadequate. Local arrangements can be made to support, and, if necessary, inspect a secondary department, or a primary Key Stage team – any parts of schools' provision about which there is evidence of concern. National inspectors are freed from the bondage of whole-school inspection and can inspect flexibly, for example, in subject provision, cross-institutional issues, inter-agency working.

Training in evaluation skills will be systematically provided for those involved. Such training will be complementary to the entitlement to staff development which teachers will have as part of the growth of an evidence-based profession. Data from all inspections will contribute to a national database, on which HMCI will draw in compiling clear and accessible Annual Reports and in offering professional advice to the government of the day and other policy-makers. All stakeholders in a school – senior managers, teachers, governors, school students, parents and others – will play a part in a rigorous and honest regular evaluation of performance. This process will be validated by the LEA: the effectiveness of the process, and the information collected, will be reported to elected members of the LEA. All involved in the process of evaluation, whether self-evaluation or external inspection, will have some responsibility for action based on the evidence of the exercise.

National, local and school educators must play their cooperative parts in the expansion and enrichment of the education system's intelligence, or what David Hargreaves (1999) has called with reference to the single institution 'the knowledge-creating school'. As John MacBeath (1999) puts it:

> This will be realised by putting into the custody of teachers approaches which they can use in their day-to-day practice. Learning and teaching improve when teachers have the tools and grasp the value of being learners in their own classrooms. Schools improve when they provide opportunities and time for teachers to share with one another. The system as a whole improves when schools are enabled to learn from one another. Government decision-making improves when policy-makers listen to teachers and are prepared to learn from them.

Michael Fullan (2000) makes a similar point in commenting on the reasons why school improvement initiatives are often not sustained:

> The key reason why reform fails to become widespread and sustained is that the infrastructure is weak, unhelpful, or working at cross purposes. By the infrastructure, I mean the next layer above whatever unit we are focusing on. In terms of successive levels, for example, a teacher cannot sustain change if he or she is working in a negative school culture. Similarly, a school can initiate and implement change, but not sustain it if it is operating in a less than helpful LEA. Likewise, an LEA cannot keep going if it works in a state or country which is not aligning and co-ordinating policies, and so on. Reform will not be deep or sustained if the infrastructure is not in place to provide the pressure and support needed to overcome inertia and to establish forces that continuously energise and support. . . . the interactive infrastructure outlined above builds in powerful 'lateral accountability' as people cannot help being

influenced, energised and rewarded for their performance, or being noticed if they fail to contribute.

(p. 15)

This 'infrastructure' of school, LEA and national government is a much more positive base from which to work for school improvement than the static and unambitious relationship which OFSTED (2000a) appears to envisage, with the LEA role being restricted to 'monitoring and necessary intervention'. The goal of the autonomous school, free from LEA intervention unless things are going wrong, misses the point: we should expect our schools constantly to be reviewing their performance and to be seeking to improve it.

I have suggested that the current system of school inspection in Scotland has much to offer those south of the border. Its quality, and its basic values, are rooted in the history of inspection during the last two centuries. Perhaps its most persuasive advocate was John Kerr, who was appointed HMI in 1860 and retired as Senior Chief Inspector in Scotland in 1896. Noting what he believed to be the destructive force of the Revised Code and Payment by Results on school standards in Scotland, he looked back on a more positive period;

> There was a delightful absence of blue pencils, standards and educational schedules . . . a teacher whose heart was in his work gave instructions under healthier conditions and with greater efficiency from feeling that he was free to do what he thought best for those under his charge; free to take account of, and adapt his teaching to, varying degrees and kinds of ability; free to minister to the capacity of those who were 'gleg at the uptak', instead of making them mark time with those of duller mood . . . [*as for teachers*] . . . I dealt with them as fellow-workers with me in a common cause, for the successful promotion of which sympathetic co-operation was essential. . . . I think of them as a most valuable class of public servants, year by year taking a higher level in culture and social position, and doing eminently useful work with praiseworthy fidelity and success, many of them for emoluments below their merits.
>
> (Kerr, quoted in Sutherland 1990)

The inspection arrangements I am proposing are neither cosy for schools nor inexpensive. They are intended to form the basis of a process, at once more rigorous and more constructive than OFSTED arrangements, which will contribute to the best possible educational provision for students in schools. I believe there are many benefits within the proposed arrangements which would also lead to a better qualified and more confident teaching profession. Schools should benefit from the high priority within the arrangements given to school improvement. The community should benefit from more reliable evidence about the state of its school system. In short, the proposed arrangements would be the key elements of a system which supports competence, rather than one which monitors incompetence.

Above all, each of us in the twenty-first century should see ourselves as learners, and all working within the education system should accept their complementary roles in providing the best possible service for all citizens. In this process, school inspectors still have a unique role in 'affording assistance'.

References

Alexander, R. (1999) 'Inspection and education: the indivisibility of standards', in C. Cullingford (ed.) *An Inspector Calls*, London: Kogan Page.

Alexander, R., Rose, J. and Woodhead, C. (1992*) Curriculum Organisation and Classroom Practice in Primary Schools*, London: Kogan Page.

Ancess, J. (1996) *Outside/inside, Inside/outside: Developing and Implementing the School Quality Review*, New York: National Center for Restructuring Education, Schools and Teaching, Teachers College, Columbia University.

Arnold, M. (1854) *Reports on Elementary Schools 1852–1882*, edited by F. S. Marvin (1908), London: Board of Education.

Baker, K. (1988) *Secretary of State's Speech to the Society of Education Officers*, 22 January, London: Department of Education and Science (DES).

Bangs, J. (1998) *LEAs and Schools: a Social Partnership*, London: TEN – The Education Network.

Barber, M. (1996) *The Learning Game: Arguments for an Educational Revolution*, London: Victor Gollancz.

Barth, R. (1990) *Improving Schools from Within*, San Francisco CA: Jossey-Bass.

Beckett, F. (1999) 'The real Chris Woodhead scandal', *New Statesman*, 26th April.

Betts, R. (1986) 'My boys did rather badly – the Silverlock case 1888', *Journal of Educational Administration and History*, 18(2): 17–23.

Birchenough, C. (1946) 'Inspectors and organisers in the educational system', Presidential address to National Association of Inspectors and Educational Advisers, in J. Dean (1991) *The First Seventy Years: A History of the National Association of Inspectors and Educational Advisers*, Haywards Heath: NAIEA.

Black, P. and Wiliam, D. (1998) *Inside the Black Box: Raising Standards Through Classroom Assessment*, London: King's College School of Education.

Board of Education (1905) 'Suggestions for the consideration of teachers and others concerned with the work of Public Elementary Schools', in S. Maclure (ed. 1965) *Educational Documents: England and Wales 1816 to the Present Day*, London: Methuen.

Board of Education (1922–23) *Annual Report.*

Bollington, R., Hopkins, D. and West, M. (1990) *An Introduction to Teacher Appraisal: a Professional Development Approach,* London: Cassell.

Bolton, E. (1998) 'HMI – the Thatcher years', *Oxford Review of Education,* 24(1).

Bone, T. R. (1968) *School Inspection in Scotland: 1840–1966,* London: London University Press.

Bottery, M. and Wright, N. (1999) *The Directed Profession: Teachers and the State in the Third Millennium.* Paper given at the SCETT Annual Conference, November, at Dunchurch, Rugby.

Brighouse, T. and Moon, B. (1995) *School Inspection,* London: Pitman Publishing.

Browne, S. (1979) 'The accountability of HM Inspectorate', in J. Lello (ed.) *Accountability,* London: Ward Lock.

Brunel University Centre for the Evaluation of Public Policy and Practice and the Helix Consulting Group (1999) *The OFSTED System of School Inspection: An Independent Evaluation,* a report commissioned by the Office for Standards in Inspection (OFSTIN).

Bryce, T. G. K. and Humes, W. M. (eds) (1999) *Scottish Education,* Edinburgh: Edinburgh University Press.

Bryk, A. and Schneider, B. (2001) *Relational Trust: a Social Resource for School Improvement.* Manuscript in preparation for American Sociological Association's 'Rose Series', New York: Russell Sage.

Burchill, J. (1991) *Inspecting Schools: Breaking the Monopoly,* London: Centre for Policy Studies.

Bush, T. (ed.) (1980) *Approaches to School Management,* London: Paul Chapman.

Callaghan, J. (1976) 'Towards a national debate', *Education,* 148(17): 334–5.

Carlton Club Political Committee (1991) Unpublished document.

Clark, P. (1998) *Back from the Brink: Transforming the Ridings School and Our Children's Education,* London: Metro.

Coleman, J., Campbell, E., Hobson, C., McPartland, J., Mood, A., Weinfeld, F. and York, R. (1966) *Equality of Educational Opportunity,* Washington DC: US Government Printing Office.

Committee of the Council of Education (1897) 'Minutes', in S. Maclure (ed. 1965) *Educational Documents: England and Wales 1816 to the Present Day,* London: Methuen.

Cordingley, P. and Kogan, M. (1993) *In Support of Education: the Functioning of Local Government,* London: Jessica Kingsley.

Costa, A. and Kallick, B. (1993) 'Through the lens of a critical friend', *Education Leadership,* 51(2): 49–51.

Council of Local Education Authorities (1997) *Local Education Authorities and Improving Schools,* London: CLEA.

Creese, M. (1997) *Effective Governance: the Evidence from OFSTED,* Ipswich: School Management and Governance Development.

Creese, M. and Earley, P. (1999) *Improving Schools and Governing Bodies*, London: Routledge.

Cullingford, C. (ed.) (1999) *An Inspector Calls: OFSTED and its Effect on School Standards*, London: Kogan Page.

Cullingford, C. and Daniels, S. (1999) 'The effects of OFSTED inspection on school performance', in C. Cullingford (ed.) *An Inspector Calls*. London: Kogan Page.

Cuttance, P. (1994) 'The contribution of quality assurance reviews to development in school systems', in D. Hargreaves and D. Hopkins (eds) *Development Planning for School Improvement*, London: Cassell.

Darling-Hammond, L. (1997) *The Right To Learn*, San Francisco CA: Jossey-Bass.

Darling-Hammond, L. and McLaughlin, M. (1995) 'Policies that support professional development in an era of reform', *Phi Delta Kappan*, 76: 597–604.

Davies, B. (1990) *Education Management for the 1990s*, London: Longman.

Deal, T. E. and Kennedy, A. (1983) 'Culture and school performance', *Educational Leadership*, 40(5): 140–1.

Department of Education and Science (DES) (1983) *The Work of HM Inspectorate in England and Wales: A Policy Statement by the Secretary of State for Education and Science and the Secretary of State for Wales*, London: HMSO.

DfEE (Department for Education and Employment) (1997) *Excellence in Schools*, London: HMSO.

DfEE (1999) *Code of Practice on School – LEA Relations*, London: DfEE.

DfEE (2000) *Professional Development: Support for Teaching and Learning*, London: The Stationery Office.

Douglas, J. (1964) *The Home and the School*, London: MacGibbon and Kee.

Duignan, P. A. and Macpherson, R. J. S. (1992) *Education Leadership: a Practical Theory for New Administrators and Managers*, London: Falmer.

Dunford, J. E. (1998) *Her Majesty's Inspectorate of Schools Since 1944: Standard Bearers or Turbulent Priests?* London: Woburn Press.

Earley, P. (1997) 'External inspections, "failing schools" and the role of governing bodies', *School Leadership and Management* 17(3).

Earley, P. (ed.) (1998) *School Improvement after Inspection*, London: Paul Chapman.

Edmonds, E. L. (1962) *The School Inspector*, London: Routledge and Kegan Paul.

Eisner, E. (1985) *The Art of Educational Evaluation*, Lewes: Falmer.

Elliott, J. (1991) *Action Research for Educational Change*, Milton Keynes: OUP.

Elmore, R. (1995) 'Getting to scale with good educational practice', *Harvard Educational Review*, 66(1): 1–26.

Eraut, M. (1992) *Developing the Professions: Training, Quality and Accountability*, Brighton: University of Sussex.

Ferguson, N., Earley, P., Fidler, B. and Ouston, J. (1999) *The Inspection of Primary*

Schools: Factors Associated with School Development, London: Nuffield Foundation/Institute of Education.

Ferguson, N., Earley, P., Fidler, B. and Ouston, J. (2000) *Improving Schools and Inspection: the Self-Inspecting School,* London: Paul Chapman.

Fidler, B., Ouston, J., Earley, P., Ferguson, N. and Davies, J. (1999) *The Inspection of Schools as a Contribution to School Improvement.* Paper presented at the International Congress on School Effectiveness and Improvement (ICSEI) in San Antonio, Texas, 3–6 January.

Field, C., Greenstreet, D., Kusel, P. and Parsons, C. (1998) 'OFSTED inspection reports and the language of educational improvement', *Evaluation and Research in Education,* 12(3).

Fisher, D. (1999) *Partnership for Progress: Support for Underachieving Schools,* Slough: NFER.

Fitz-Gibbon, C. and Stephenson-Forster, N. (1999) 'Is OFSTED helpful?', in C. Cullingford (ed.) *An Inspector Calls,* London: Kogan Page.

Frost, D. (1997) *Reflective Action Planning for Teachers: A Guide to Teacher-led School and Professional Development,* London: David Fulton.

Frost, D., Durrant, J., Head, M. and Holden, G. (2000) *Teacher-Led School Improvement,* London: RoutledgeFalmer.

Fullan, M. G. (1991) with Steigelbaum, S. *The New Meaning of Educational Change,* New York: Teachers College Press, and London: Cassell.

Fullan, M. G. (1992) *Successful School Improvement,* Buckingham: Open University Press and Toronto: OISE Press.

Fullan, M. G. (2000) 'Infrastructure is all', *Times Educational Supplement,* 23 June.

Fullan, M. and Hargreaves, A. (1992) *What's Worth Fighting for in Your School?* Buckingham: Open University Press.

Gewirtz, S., Ball, S. J. and Bowe, R. (1995) *Markets, Choice and Equality in Education,* Buckingham: Open University Press.

Goleman, D. (1996) *Emotional Intelligence: Why it Matters More than IQ,* London: Bloomsbury.

Grace, G. (1995) *School Leadership: Beyond Educational Management,* London: Falmer.

Grace, G. (1999) *Teacher Education and Professionalism.* Lecture given at Canterbury Christ Church University College, 22 June.

Gray, J. (1998) *The Contribution of Educational Research to the Course of School Improvement,* London: Institute of Education.

Gray, J. and Hannon, V. (1986) 'HMI interpretation of schools' examination results', *Journal of Education Policy* 1: 23–33.

Gray, J. and Wilcox, B. (1995) 'Inspection and school improvement: rhetoric and experience from the bridge', in J. Gray and B. Wilcox (eds) *'Good School, Bad School': Evaluating Performance and Encouraging Improvement,* Buckingham: Open University Press.

Gray, J., Hopkins, D., Reynolds, D., Wilcox, B., Farrell, S. and Jesson, D. (1999) *Improving Schools: Performance and Potential*, Buckingham: OUP.

Green, D. (1997) *A Field Guide to Inquiry* (First draft), New York: School Change Through Inquiry Project.

Greenwald, R., Hedges, L. and Laine, R. (1996) 'The effect of school resources on student achievement', *Review of Educational Research*, 66(3): 361–96.

Hargreaves, D. (1995a) 'Inspection and school improvement', *Cambridge Journal of Education*, 25(1): 117–25.

Hargreaves, D. (1995b) 'Self managing schools and development planning', *School Organisation* 15(3): 226.

Hargreaves, D. (1999) 'Helping practitioners explore their school's culture', in J. Prosser (ed.) *School Culture*, London: Paul Chapman.

Hayward, F. H. (1912) *Educational Administration and Criticism*, London: Ralph & Holland.

Hopkins, D., Ainscow, M. and West, M. (1994) *School Improvement in an Era of Change*, London: Cassell.

House of Commons Education and Employment Committee (1999a) *The Work of OFSTED*, Fourth Report, London: The Stationery Office.

House of Commons Education and Employment Committee (1999b) *Government's and OFSTED's Response to the Fourth Committee, Session 1998–1999: The work of OFSTED*, Fifth Special Report, London: The Stationery Office.

Hughes, M. (2000) 'Crossing the river', *The Enquirer – CANTARNET Journal* (Summer).

Institution for School and College Governors (1996) *Inspection – a Weapon or a Tool, a Post-mortem or a Health Check?* London: ISCG.

Jenkins, V. (1987) *School Effectiveness and School Change: The IBIS Approach*. Paper presented to Annual Conference of BERA at Manchester Polytechnic.

Johnson, M. (1999) *Failing School, Failing City*, Charlbury, Oxon: Jon Carpenter.

Joyce, B. R. (1991) 'The doors to school improvement', *Educational Leadership*, 48(8): 59–62.

Joyce, B. R. and Showers, B. (1982) 'The coaching of teaching', *Educational Leadership*, 40(2): 4–10.

Joyce, B., Calhoun, E., and Hopkins, D. (1997) *Models of Learning: Tools for Teaching*, Buckingham: OUP.

Kogan, M. (1996) *Developing LEA Commissioned Evaluations*. Address to Standing Conference of Chief Education Officers, University of Warwick.

Kozol, J. (1991) *Savage Inequalities*, New York: Crown Publishing.

Lauder, H., Jamieson, I. and Wikeley, F. (1998) 'Models of effectiveness: limits and capacities' in R. Slee, S. Tomlinson, with G. Weiner (eds) *School Effectiveness for Whom?* London: Falmer.

Law, S. and Glover, D. (1999) 'Does Ofsted make a difference? Inspection issues and socially deprived schools', in C. Cullingford (ed.) *An Inspector Calls*, London: Kogan Page.

Lawlor, H. and Sills, P. (1999) 'Successful leadership – evidence from highly effective headteachers', *Improving Schools* 2(2), Stoke-on-Trent: Trentham Books.

Lawton, D. and Gordon, P. (1987) *HMI*, London: Routledge and Kegan Paul.

Leithwood, K. and Louis, K. S. (1998) *Organisational Learning in Schools*, Lisse: Swets and Zeitlinger.

Levacic, R. (1999) *New Labour Policy in the United Kingdom: 'The Third Way'*. Paper presented at a research seminar conducted by Centre for Applied Educational Research, University of Melbourne, Australia.

Levacic, R. and Glover, D. (1994) *OFSTED Assessment of Schools' Efficiency: an Analysis of 66 Secondary School Inspection Reports*, Milton Keynes: Open University, Centre for Educational Policy and Management.

Lister, E. (1991) *LEAs Old and New*, London: Centre for Policy Studies.

Lodge, C. (1998) 'What's wrong with our schools? Understanding "ineffective" and "failing schools"', in L. Stoll and K. Myers (eds) *No Quick Fixes: Perspectives on Schools in Difficulty*, London: Falmer Press.

Lonsdale, P. and Parsons, C. (1998) 'Inspection and the school improvement hoax', in P. Earley (ed.) *School Improvement After Inspection*, London: Paul Chapman.

Louis, K. S. and Miles, M. B. (1990) *Improving the Urban High School: What Works and Why*, New York: Teachers College Press and (1991) London: Cassell.

Lowe, R. (1862) *Revised Code of Regulations*, London: The Committee of the Privy Council on Education.

MacBeath, J. (1999) *Schools Must Speak for Themselves: The Case for School Self-evaluation*, London: Routledge.

MacBeath, J. and Myers, K. (1999) *Effective School Leaders: How to Evaluate and Improve Your Leadership Potential*, Harlow: Pearson.

MacBeath, J., Boyd, B., Rand, J. and Bell, S. (1996) *Schools Speak for Themselves*, London: NUT.

McCall, C. (1998) *School Self Review Manual*, London: Financial Times.

McClelland, D. (1987) *Human Motivation*, Cambridge: Cambridge University Press.

McGlynn, A. and Stalker, H. (1995) 'Recent developments in the Scottish process of school inspection', *Cambridge Journal of Education* 25(1): 13–23.

Maclure, S. (1979) *Educational Documents: England and Wales 1816 to 1968*, London: Methuen and Co.

McMahon, A., Bolam, R., Abbott, R. and Holly, P. (1984) *Guidelines for Review and Internal Development in Schools*, (Primary and Secondary School Handbooks), York: Longman/Schools Council.

McNeil, F. (1999) 'Brain research and learning – an introduction', *School Improvement Network Research Matters,* London: Institute of Education.

Maeroff, G. (1998) *Altered Destinies,* New York: Martin's Griffin.

Maw, J. (1995) *The Handbook for the Inspection of Schools: a Critique,* London: Institute of Education.

Maychell, K. and Keys, W. (1993) *Under Inspection: LEA Evaluation and Monitoring,* Slough: National Foundation for Educational Research.

Maychell, K. and Pathak, S. (1997) *Planning for Action Part 1: A Survey of Schools' Post-inspection Action Planning,* Slough: NFER.

Miles, M. and Ekholm, M. (1985) 'What is school improvement?', in W. Van Velzen, M. Miles, M., Ekholm, U. Haneyer, and D. Robin, (eds) *Making School Improvement Work: A Conceptual Guide to Practice,* Leven, Belgium: ACCO.

Mortimore, P. (1998) *The Road to Improvement: Reflections on School Effectiveness,* Lisse, Netherlands: Swets and Zeitlinger.

Mortimore, P. (2000) *Globalisation, Effectiveness and Improvement.* Presentation to International Congress for School Effectiveness and Improvement (ICSEI), Hong Kong.

Mortimore, P. and Whitty, G. (1997) *Can School Improvement Overcome the Effects of Disadvantage?* London: Institute of Education, University of London.

Mortimore, P., Sammons, P., Stoll, L., Lewis, D. and Ecob, R. (1988) *School Matters: The Junior Years,* Somerset: Open University Press.

Myers, K. (1996) *School Improvement in Practice: Schools Make a Difference,* London: Falmer.

Myers, K. and Goldstein, H. (1998) 'Who's failing?' in L. Stoll and K. Myers (eds) *No Quick Fixes: Perspectives on Schools in Difficulty,* London: Falmer.

National Association of Head Teachers (NAHT) (1999) *School Self-Review,* Secondary Leadership, Paper No.3.

National Commission on Education (1996) *Success Against the Odds: Effective Schools in Disadvantaged Areas,* London: Routledge.

O'Connor, M., Hales, E., Davies, J. and Tomlinson, S. (1999) *Hackney Downs, the School that Dared to Fight,* London: Cassell.

OFSTED (1993) *Access and Achievement in Urban Education,* London: HMSO.

OFSTED (1994) *Improving Schools,* London: HMSO.

OFSTED (1995) *Framework for the Inspection of Schools,* London: OFSTED.

OFSTED (1996) *Schools in the Manningham Area of Bradford,* London: OFSTED.

OFSTED (1997a) *From Failure to Success: How Special Measures Are Helping Schools Improve,* London: OFSTED.

OFSTED (1997b) *National Curriculum Assessment Results and the Wider Curriculum at Key Stage 2: Some Evidence from the OFSTED Database,* London: OFSTED/DfEE.

OFSTED (1998a) *Secondary Education, 1993–97,* London: OFSTED.

OFSTED (1998b) *School Evaluation Matters*, London: OFSTED.

OFSTED (1998c) *Inspection Quality 1996–7: Schools' Views of Inspection*, London: OFSTED.

OFSTED (1999) *Lessons Learned from Special Measures*, London: OFSTED.

OFSTED (2000a) *Inspecting Schools: the Framework*, London: OFSTED.

OFSTED (2000b) *Improving City Schools*, London: OFSTED.

OFSTED (2000c) *Local Education Authority Support for School Improvement: A Draft Paper for Consultation*, London: OFSTED.

OFSTED (2000d) *Chief Inspector's Annual Report, 1998–9*, London: OFSTED.

OFSTIN (1997) *A Better System of Inspection?* Hexham: The Office for Standards in Inspection.

Olson, L. (1994) 'Critical friends', *Education Week* 13(32): 27.

Ouston, J. and Davies, J. (1998) 'OFSTED and afterwards: schools' responses to inspection', in P. Earley (ed.) *School Improvement After Inspection? School and LEA Responses*. London. Paul Chapman.

Ouston, J. and Klenowski, V. (1995) *The Ofsted Experience: The Parents' Eye View*, London: Research and Information on State Education Trust (RISE).

Phillips, M. (1996) *All Must Have Prizes*, London: Little, Brown and Company.

Pickering, J. (1997) 'Involving pupils', in *School Improvement Network Research Matters*, London: Institute of Education.

Power, M. *et al.* (1967) 'Delinquent schools', *New Society* 10: 542–3.

Radnor, H. and Ball, S. (1996) *Local Education Authorities: Accountability and Control*, Stoke-on-Trent: Trentham Books.

Reed, J. and Learmonth, J. (2000) *Revitalising Teachers' Accountability: Learning About Learning as a Renewed Focus for School Improvement*. Paper presented at Thirteenth International Congress for School Effectiveness and Improvement (ICSEI), Hong Kong.

Reeves, J., Moos, L. and Forrest, J. (1998) 'The school leader's view', in J. MacBeath (ed.) *Effective School Leadership*, London: Paul Chapman.

Reynolds, D. (1976) 'The delinquent school', in M. Hammersley and P. Woods (eds) *The Process of Schooling*, London: Routledge and Kegan Paul.

Reynolds, D. (1995) 'Some very peculiar practices', *Times Educational Supplement*, 16 June.

Reynolds, D. (1998) 'British school improvement research: the contribution of qualitative studies', *International Journal of Qualitative Studies in Education*.

Reynolds, D. and Stoll, L. (1996) 'Managing school effectiveness and school improvement: the knowledge base', in D. Reynolds (ed.) *Making Good Schools*, London: Routledge.

Ribbins, P. and Burridge, E. (eds) (1994) *Improving Education: Promoting Quality in Schools*, London: Cassell.

Rhode Island Department of Education (RIDE) (1999) *SALTWORKS School by*

School: A School-centred Plan to Improve Teaching and Learning, Book 1. Rhode Island: Rhode Island Department of Education.

Riley, K. (1998) *Whose School Is It Anyway?* London: Falmer Press.

Riley, K. and Rowles, D. (1997) *Learning from Failure,* London: Haringey Council.

RISE (1994) *The Ofsted Experience – A Governor's Eye View,* London: Research and Information on State Education Trust.

Robertson, P. and Sammons, P. (1997) *The Improving School Effectiveness Project (ISEP): Understanding Change in Schools.* Paper presented at BERA, University of York.

Rogers, G. *et al.* (1977) *Keeping the School Under Review,* London: Inner London Education Authority.

Rosenholtz, S. J. (1989) *Teachers' Workplace: the Social Organisation of Schools,* New York: Longman.

Ruddock, J., Chaplain, R. and Wallace, G. (eds) (1996) *School Improvement: What Can Pupils Tell Us?* London: David Fulton.

Russell, S. (1996) *Collaborative School Self Review,* London: Lemos and Crane.

Rutter, M., Maughan, B., Mortimore, P. and Ouston, J. (1979) *Fifteen Thousand Hours: Secondary Schools and Their Effects on Schoolchildren,* Shepton Mallet: Open Books.

Sammons, P., Hillman, J. and Mortimore, P. (1995) *Key Characteristics of Effective Schools: a Review of School Effectiveness Research,* London: Office for Standards in Education (OFSTED).

Sammons, P., Thomas, S. and Mortimore, P. (1997) *Forging Links: Effective Schools and Effective Departments,* London: Paul Chapman.

Sammons, P., Taggart, B. and Thomas, S. (1998) *Making Belfast Work: Raising School Standards,* London: ISEIC, Institute of Education.

Sandbrook, I. (1996) *Making Sense of Primary Inspection,* Buckingham: Open University Press.

Sarason, S. (1982) *The Culture of the School and the Problem of Change,* Boston: Allyn and Bacon.

Scanlon, M. (1999) *The Impact of OFSTED Inspections,* London: NUT/NFER.

Scheerens, J. *et al* (1999) 'Aspects of the organizational and political context of school evaluation in four European countries', in *Studies in Educational Evaluation,* 25: 79–108.

Schein, E. H. (1985) *Organizational Culture and Leadership,* San Francisco, CA: Jossey-Bass.

Schon, D. (1983) *The Reflective Practitioner: How Professionals Think in Action,* New York: Basic Books.

Senge, P. (1990) *The Fifth Discipline: the Art and Practice of the Learning Organisation,* New York: Currency Doubleday.

Shaw, M., Brimblecombe, N. and Ormston, M. (1995) 'It ain't what you do, it's the way that you do it', *Management in Education,* 9 (1).

Singleton, D. (1998) 'LEA inspections: the reality behind the rhetoric,' in *Education*, 26 (September).

Stark, M. (1998) 'No slow fixes either: how failing schools in England are being restored to health', in L. Stoll and K. Myers (eds) *No Quick Fixes: Perspectives on Schools in Difficulty*, London: Falmer Press.

Stoll, L. and Mortimore, P. (1995) 'School effectiveness and school improvement', *Viewpoint 2*. London: ISEIC, Institute of Education.

Stoll, L. and Fink, D. (1996) *Changing Our Schools*, Buckingham: Open University Press.

Stoll, L. and Thomson, M. (1996) 'Moving together: a partnership approach to improvement,' in P. Earley, B. Fidler and J. Ouston (eds) *Improvement Through Inspection: Complementary Approaches to School Development*, London: David Fulton.

Sutherland, M. B. (1990) *HMIs and Education in Scotland*, Edinburgh: Scottish Education Department.

Teddlie, C. and Stringfield, S. (1993) *Schools Make a Difference: Lessons Learned from a 10 Year Study of School Effects*, New York: Teachers College Press.

Thompson, F. (1945) *Lark Rise to Candleford*, Harmondsworth: Penguin.

Thomson, C. W. (1936) *Scottish School Humour*, Glasgow: Robert Gibson and Sons.

Thrupp, M. (1999) *Schools Making a Difference: Let's be Realistic*, Buckingham: Open University Press.

Tooley, J. (2000) *Reclaiming Education*, London: Cassell.

Tooley, J. and Darby, D. (1998) *Educational Research: A Critique*, London. OFSTED.

Victorian Commission of Audit (1993) *School Evaluation*, Victoria, Australia: VCA.

Watling, R., Hopkins, D., Harris, A. and Beresford, J. (1998) 'Between the devil and the deep blue sea? Implications for school and LEA development following an accelerated inspection programme', in L. Stoll and K. Myers (eds) *No Quick Fixes: Perspectives on Schools in Difficulty*, London: Falmer.

Wilcox, B. (1992) *Time Constrained Evaluation*, London: Routledge.

Wilcox, B. and Gray, J. (1994) 'Reactions to inspection: a study of three variants', *Cambridge Journal of Education* 24: 245–59.

Wilcox, B., Gray, J. and Tranmer, M. (1993) 'LEA frameworks for the assessment of schools: an interrupted picture', *Educational Research*, 35(3): 211–21.

Wilson, T. (1996) *Reaching for a Better Standard*, New York: Teachers College.

Wilson, T. (2000) *Handbook for Chairs of the SALT School Visit*, Providence, RI: Rhode Island Department of Education/CATALPA.

Woodhead, C. (1998) 'Blood on the tracks', HMCI's Annual Lecture, London: OFSTED.

Wragg, E. and Brighouse, T. (1995) *A New Model of School Inspection*, Exeter: Exeter University School of Education.

Appendix

This Appendix contains summaries of two substantial reviews of OFSTED's work. They are included because they are substantial and important documents, not readily accessible to the widest possible audience.

The OFSTED System of School Inspection: An Independent Evaluation, published by Brunel University Centre for the Evaluation of Public Policy and Practice and the Helix Consulting Group in 1999. The report was commissioned by the Office for Standards in Inspection (OFSTIN)

Key findings

Schools and national associations feel that schools should be accountable and inspected

Preparing for inspection makes too heavy demands on schools

- The period of build-up leads to 'anticipatory dread', interferes with normal school development work and impairs teaching effectiveness.
- It emphasises OFSTED-related paperwork and the physical presentation of the school.

Relationships between the inspectors and the school are crucial

- All these relationships are highly dependent upon the registered inspector.
- Registered inspectors should know the team's strengths and have the ability to manage the team and the inspection process.
- Head-teachers mostly find them professional and focused on management; teachers report variation and inconsistency.
- Contact between inspectors and governors and parents is kept to the minimum statutory requirements.

Key factors affecting the experience of inspection

- The perceived lack of credibility and professionalism of the members of the team.
- The manner in which the inspection is conducted.
- Lack of faith in the reliability and validity of the process.
- Classroom observation lacks credibility among teachers because of the criteria by which teachers/classes to be observed are selected; the subject expertise of the inspectors; the judgement and grades assigned to teachers' performance; and a range of errors in the administration of the scheme at school level.

Schools value the inspection feedback

- It is seen as fair, valid and of good standard except that given to teachers about their teaching performance.
- Schools would prefer feedback to be an aid to professional and school development.

The inspection reports and key issues identified

- Most head-teachers, teachers, governors and parents, accept the key issues as fair and relevant.
- However, they are not always seen as the most important for the schools and in some cases are relatively trivial.
- In other cases, there are no resources available to the school to address the key issues identified.

- The reports do not tell the schools anything they do not know already and sometimes inspection misses real problems.
- For staff and governors, the reports are mostly consistent with the feedback given at the end of the inspection week.
- The overall judgements are seen to be valid and fair, with governors and parents more strongly accepting.
- Parents are reassured by the judgement of 'good' schools but likely to dismiss reports critical of 'their' school.
- The usefulness of the summary report for parents is doubtful and few parents read the full report.
- The factual accuracy of some reports, and the lack of opportunity to challenge errors of fact, is an issue.
- The reports are not seen to make much difference to the schools or to aid the further development of schools.

Outcomes and impacts of the inspection process

- Action plans are seen mainly as a formality to be completed at the end of the inspection process.
- Generally most of the actions required are seen to be covered already in existing school development plans.
- Concern is expressed by national associations that existing school development plans are disrupted by the requirement for an action plan.
- The impact of inspection on failing schools is acknowledged but the benefits for better schools are less agreed.
- Some changes in organisational structure and some of the improvements reported by schools on a range of performance indicators are attributed to inspection.
- Changes in staff, some of which are detrimental to schools, are also attributed to the inspection process.
- The OFSTED framework is considered to assist school improvement perhaps more than the inspection itself.
- Schools felt that they are more focused and rigorous in school development activities as a result of inspection.
- Governors rather than teachers or head-teachers are more likely to ascribe performance improvements to inspection.
- On OFSTED's own performance criteria, inspection is judged to have had an impact in only a minority of schools.

Schools' reflections and evaluations

- Schools and others identify the potential value of external perspectives on the work and management of schools.
- The pre-inspection self-evaluation; public affirmation of good performance; and the increase in school collegiality are seen as benefits of the lead-up to inspection.
- Inspection can lead to greater clarity about roles and responsibilities particularly among governors.
- Overall, the system is seen as punitive and fault findings, which 'celebrates faults rather than the success' and generates a climate of fear leading to stress, anxiety and infantilism among teaching staff.
- Parents recognise benefits in the system but also the adverse impacts on staff, which leads to concern about the impacts of the inspection process on their children.

Strengths of the system

- The clear framework, which promotes improved management systems and structures. This can be used by schools as a valuable aid to self-development.
- The systematic form of the inspection process which can result in greater rigour in self-assessment and evaluation.
- The same framework and process can be applied to all schools.
- Governors (though not school staff) are more likely to see the inspection process as a catalyst for change.
- Parents see inspection as leading to improvements within the school their own children attend.

Weaknesses of the system

- It promotes a management model that is outdated.
- The summative, judgemental outcomes are not effective in promoting reflective professional development within schools.
- The system is intolerant of alternative approaches to school improvement and effectiveness.

Accountability and national standards

- Most governors feel that accountability is improved but this view is shared by virtually no head-teachers or teachers.
- National associations express misgivings about the OFSTED model for achieving greater accountability.
- Head-teachers, teachers and governors are cautious about the potential positive role of OFSTED in raising national educational standards, though parents are more positive.
- The policy of 'naming and shaming' was felt to be counter-productive.
- The current arrangements do not contribute to the reduction in the number of ineffectual teachers.
- It is not appropriate for the issue of poor teachers to be dealt with through current OFSTED arrangements.
- National associations are strongly in support of different arrangements for identifying and dealing with poor teachers.

The costs of school inspections

- The majority of head-teachers, teachers, governors, parents, LEA and national representatives interviewed and surveyed do not believe that OFSTED school inspection offers value for money.
- The calculation of the costs of school inspection should include those incurred at school, LEA and national level, and opportunity as well as direct and indirect costs.
- The OFSTED costs for inspections for median size secondary schools are over £27,000; over £9,000 for primary and nursery schools; and over £19,000 for special schools. Contracted school inspection costs over £92 million with £28 million associated other costs.
- The average additional cost to schools amount to a minimum of 1–3 per cent of the total school budget. Indirect costs, including opportunity costs are probably greater. Twenty per cent of additional teacher time is taken up with OFSTED related preparation in the three months before inspection.
- LEAs spend £550–900 a school on pre-inspection assistance. They spend £900–£1,450 on post-inspection work with primary and £1,450 to £1,810 on secondary schools.

- The total costs (excluding opportunity costs) for a median size primary school are £26,020 (4.5 per cent of school budget) and £65,893 (3.2 per cent of school budget) for a median size secondary school.
- Cost analyses should be applied on a regular basis to OFSTED.

Policy and practice implications: a revised system of school inspection?

- An achievement of the OFSTED system of school inspection is that it has promoted acceptance of a 'culture of inspection'.
- Current inspection arrangements make too heavy workload and associated emotional demands on school personnel.
- The costs, financial and otherwise, are not seen as value for money in terms of either school performance of pupil achievement.
- The system is seen as punitive and adversarial and not contributing to formative professional or school development. On the contrary, it is leading towards a form of dependent infantilism within the teaching profession.
- It should involve a professional, reflective dialogue between professionals ascribed equal status in the procedure.
- Inspection should be tied to professional staff development and rigorous staff appraisal.
- There is a key role in this revised system to be played by LEAs.
- Contracting out to competing, peripatetic, journeymen inspectors does not produce the interaction between professionals required for continuing school improvement because informed reflective professional dialogue is based upon accumulated knowledge, expertise and the dissemination of good practice. The case for an established *cadre of inspectors* is made.
- In terms of school improvement and effectiveness the system focuses too much upon school and teacher performance rather than pupil achievement and the 'non-school' factors which have been shown to affect this.
- There is a range of policy and practice implications for national government, OFSTED, schools, local authorities, parent and governor associations, and teacher associations. Inspection should be more developmental in its mode of operation with strong elements of self-evaluation and peer review.

The Work of OFSTED: A report from the House of Commons Education Sub-Committee (1999)
London: Stationery Office

Overview

External inspection of schools by national government has a long history, beginning with the first inspections by HM Inspectors of Schools in 1839. The establishment of OFSTED, as a result of the Education (Schools) Act 1992, significantly increased the number of schools inspected each year. The subsequent development of OFSTED's inspection system has generated a degree of controversy, often accompanied by a high media profile. However, it is important to remember that the development of OFSTED reflects a growing expectation on the part of the public that public services will be more directly answerable to those who use them. This is part of the development of an 'audit society', and education is no exception. We based our inquiry on our support for thorough, independent, external inspection of education services in England, which was shared by our witnesses. The key test of effective inspection is the extent to which it enables the education of children.

School inspections

School inspections are carried out by independent inspectors working for approved contracting organisations. The current process does not provide sufficient incentives for high-quality contractors and we recommend that OFSTED should consider whether the rates of pay are driving the highest quality inspectors out of school inspections. OFSTED's Inspection Framework for schools was widely praised in the inquiry. However, it needs to be applied in a way which takes account of the varying aims of the different kinds of special schools. The Inspection Framework should also take better account of the challenges facing schools with high levels of pupil mobility.

Inspection is, for many schools, a stressful experience. We were provided with examples of inspections which had negative effect on teachers and this, we have no doubt, has contributed to what one of described as the 'demonisation' of the OFSTED process. iousness of these cases, but note that the majority of spection teams to be professional and courteous. We believe the period of notice of inspection which is provided to schools is too long and should normally be four working weeks. Reducing the period of notice in this way would benefit schools as it would reduce the time for schools to assemble unnecessary and irrelevant masses of paper and also reduce the amount of time teachers have to develop 'anticipatory dread' of the forthcoming inspection.

The amount of feedback given to teachers and head-teachers by the inspection team has improved significantly since the inception of OFSTED inspections. We endorse the efforts made by OFSTED to enhance this aspect of the inspection process. We do not agree with those witnesses who argued that OFSTED inspectors should always provide advice *per se* based on their inspection findings. Neither do we believe that schools are best served by the 'pure audit' model of inspection. There is a broad spectrum of activity stretching from detailed advice – telling the school what to do – at one end, a wholly 'hands-off' audit at the other. The point along this spectrum at which inspectors should work will depend on the individual circumstances of the school. A more confident school may require a response from their inspection team which is closer to the 'audit' end of this spectrum, while other schools may benefit from a response which is closer to the 'advice' end. OFSTED inspectors can act best as catalyst for change and improvement. This, we believe, can best be achieved through the development of a 'professional dialogue' in which the potential benefits of inspection are realised.

Improving the inspection system

We have considered a number of possible changes to the school inspection system to maximise the benefits that inspection can bring. We do not believe it would be appropriate to conduct inspections without any notice period. On the other hand, we believe that public confidence in the education system would be enhanced if a mechanism existed for unannounced visits to schools by external agencies such as HMI or LEAs. We do not believe that it would be appropriate for schools to nominate a member of staff to the inspection team, but we do believe that there would be merit in allowing the governing body to nominate an observer who would shadow the work of the inspection team.

The role of self-evaluation in schools was a recurring theme during our evidence. We believe that effective self-evaluation by schools has an important part to play in improving standards and quality in education. However, we disagree with those who argue that it could replace external inspection of schools. To ensure its importance as a tool for school improvement, we recommend that inspectors be required to take account of the self-evaluation procedures used by school. We recognise the benefits of serving teachers undertaking OFSTED inspection, and we recommend increasing the number of teachers who train as OFSTED inspectors and who conduct occasional inspections. Lay inspectors bring a valuable perspective to the work of inspection teams. In particular, they can often bring the parent's perspective to the inspection, asking a key question: is this a school which I would wish to send my child to?

Inspection of initial teacher training

Much of the evidence we received about OFSTED's inspection of initial teacher training was critical. Teacher training providers argued that the frequency of inspection was excessive and did not contribute to high standards. As a matter of priority, consideration should be given to implementing a differentiated system of inspection for initial teacher training providers, with high-quality assurance arrangements in higher education. We recommend that the Department for Education and Employment consider ways in which inspection and quality assurance system for teacher training institutions can be rationalised.

Inspection of local education authorities

We fully support the principle of inspection of LEAs by OFSTED. We recommend that OFSTED consider ways in which a system of differentiated inspection could be introduced for LEAs on the lines currently being proposed for schools. We also believe there would be merit, over time, in broadening the scope of the inspection framework, which is currently limited to LEA's support for school improvement.

The OFSTED Complaints Adjudicator (OCA)

We welcome the establishment of the OCA, but we are concerned that the appointment procedure for the OCA does not reinforce the independence of the post. The appointment and re-appointment of the OCA should be made by a body other than OFSTED. Consideration should also be given to the feasibility of extending the OCA's role to cover other inspections carried out by OFSTED.

OFSTED's status and its accountability

The status of OFSTED as a non-ministerial government department is unique in the field of education. We do not accept the arguments put to us that OFSTED has *no* mechanisms by which it is held accountable. However, we are less sure whether these measures are working in a clear, effective and sufficient manner. This is not a criticism of OFSTED itself: OFSTED operates within the statutory framework which Parliament gave it. However, we believe it is in the best interests of education, and OFSTED itself, that stronger, clearer mechanisms be introduced. These mechanisms should not compromise OFSTED's independence – this must underpin all its work.

We believe that Parliament should play a more active role in scrutinising OFSTED's work. Therefore we recommend that a regular debate be held in the House of HMCI's annual report. Such debates could be preceded by oral evidence from HM Chief Inspector to this Committee. It is also our intention to hold regular annual meetings with HM Chief Inspector, not only on his annual report but on the work of OFSTED itself. We also believe that Parliament should be given an advisory role in the appointment or re-appointment of HM Chief Inspector. We recommend that the Chief Inspector should continue to be appointed by the Crown on the advice of the Prime Minister, as at present, but before the appointment (or re-appointment) was confirmed, this Select Committee should be given the opportunity to take evidence in public from the nominee and report to Parliament on the proposed appointment. A debate could then be held in the House on the Committee's report.

We believe that a case can be made for establishing a board of commissioners, or a supervisory or advisory board for OFSTED. Such a board, if established, should not be too large. The functions of such a board would have to be very carefully delineated in order to ensure that the Chief Inspector and other OFSTED inspectors retained full independence in their judgements. The arguments for and against establishing a board of some kind are finely balanced. We recommend that strong consideration be given to the establishment of such a board.

The role of HM Chief Inspector

The purpose of our inquiry has been to consider the work of OFSTED itself: the principle and practice of inspection. Based on the evidence we received, however, we realised that any such study would be difficult to divorce from the style adopted by Mr Chris Woodhead in his role as HM Chief Inspector.

It has not been possible for us to judge objectively Mr Woodhead's assertion that OFSTED's achievements would have been less if he had adopted a more conciliatory, even-handed style. Looking forward, it is our firm view that as OFSTED moves through the second cycle of school inspections, and builds on its work in other areas, the case for a period of consolidation is very strong. This should be reflected in the style of leadership employed by HM Chief Inspector.

Some witnesses noted the 'widespread perception' that some of Mr Woodhead's views are based more on his opinions than on inspection evidence. We have found it difficult to reach a balanced judgement based on the arguments put to us. But it is our firmly held view that it is of the highest importance that HM Chief Inspector's advice to Ministers, and his commentary on education in print, in public lectures and elsewhere, can be backed up by the inspection evidence gathered by OFSTED. It is important for OFSTED to seek balanced media coverage in whatever way it can. We do not feel that it has been successful in that respect. Therefore, we look to OFSTED to take increased responsibility for ensuring media coverage of its work focuses on the full breadth of its inspection findings.

We believe that the following principles are central to the work of the Chief Inspector:

- First, the role of the Chief Inspector should include encouraging the formation of a consensus about the importance of OFSTED's work across a wide field.
- Second, we support the view that HM Chief Inspector should, where appropriate, speak out on education issues. However, we feel strongly that such public expression of views should be based firmly

on clear and scientific evidence emerging from inspections undertaken by OFSTED's inspectors and other reputable sources.

- Third, in carrying out his or her role the Chief Inspector should be concerned to improve morale and promote confidence in the teaching profession.

Index

Note: most entries refer to inspections. This term is generally omitted as a qualifier